FISHER FOLK-LORE

The Pilgrim's Guide to Franciscan Italy (1927)
Fishing Boats and Fisher Folk on the East Coast of Scotland (1930)
Fishermen and Fishing Ways (1931)
Mariners of Brittany (1931)
The Quest of Solitude (1932)
Six Pilgrims' Sketch Books (1934)
A Pilgrim Artist in Palestine (1934)
The Catholic Church in Modern Scotland (1937)
The Caravan Pilgrim (1938)
The Scottish Fisheries—Are they doomed? (1939)
The Benedictines of Caldey (1940)
How to draw ships (1941)
British Sea Fishermen (1944)
Harbour Head—Maritime Memories (1945)
A Roving Recluse—More Memories (1946)
The Apostleship of the Sea in England and Wales (1946)
The Sea Apostolate in Ireland (1946)
Churches—their Plan and Furnishing (1948)
The Church and the Sailor (1949)
The Religious Orders and Congregations of Great Britain and Ireland (1950)
Scots Fisher Folk (1951)
Christ and the Sailor (1954)
The Call of the Cloister (1955—4th revised edition 1964)
These Made Peace (with Cecily Hallack, 1957)
The Hermit of Cat Island (1958)
Abbot Extraordinary (1958)
A Monastery in Moray (1959)
Fashions in Church Furnishings (1960)
The Brothers of Braemore (1960)
Bishops at Large (1964)
The Call of the Desert (1964)
The Building of Churches (1964)
The Art of the Church (with Iris Conlay, 1964)

PETER F. ANSON

Fisher Folk-Lore

OLD CUSTOMS, TABOOS AND SUPERSTITIONS
AMONG FISHER FOLK, ESPECIALLY IN BRITTANY
AND NORMANDY, AND ON THE EAST COAST OF
SCOTLAND

THE FAITH PRESS
7 Tufton Street London SW1

PRINTED IN GREAT BRITAIN
in 10pt. *Times type*
BY THE FAITH PRESS LTD
LEIGHTON BUZZARD

FOREWORD

'Folk Traditions die Hard' was the caption given by *The Scotsman* to a report from its Science Correspondent on Mr. Peter Opie's presidential address to the anthropology section of the British Association at Aberdeen on September 9, 1963. Mr. Opie had put the following questions to a packed audience: why do some people throw coins whenever they see a pool of water; why do some people believe that they can charm rats and mice away simply by talking to them? His answer seemed to be a general one; people go on doing things often because they have been doing them in the past—or because it is thought they have.

Exactly 1,000 years ago, said Mr. Opie, people were advised against the heresy of worshipping fountains. 'To-day it scarcely matters which spring, well, pool or fountain we visit, we find the nation obsessed by the idea that it should lighten its pocket whenever it sees contained water.' Even as he was delivering his address, Mr. Opie reported, there was 5s. lying at the bottom of the old fountain at King's College, Aberdeen. He had comfort to those among us who fear that tradition is dying out. He believed, indeed, that in many fields—such as children's stories, and the imagining of illness—we are actually generating more folk-lore than our parents and grandparents. He instanced 'the most recent story to have gone around'—that air hostesses making regular flights in high-flying aircraft are liable to become sterile. More recently a Sunday newspaper with a nation-wide circulation has published a series of articles on the witches alleged to be performing both black and white magic in Britain. This led to a question being asked in Parliament if the laws against witchcraft, repealed in 1736, could not be revived in a modified form.[1]

So it appears that folk-lore is still a force. While retaining ancient characteristics, it is adapting itself to changes in ways of living and environment. Some customs have withered away and their memory has become romantic to us. Others have prospered to such an extent that they are ordinary, even tawdry and occasionally commercialized. Folk-lore can be of value, both in exploring the past and in understanding the development of man's mind, but its importance can only be recognized when scholarly critical standards have been exercised.

[1] It was at Dornoch, capital of Sutherland, that the last British witch was burnt alive in 1722. But as recently as 1895 a reputed witch suffered the same death penalty in Co. Tipperary. Her husband and accomplices were sentenced to long terms of imprisonment.

7

What has been the attitude of the Christian Church towards taboos and superstitions in general? The word 'superstition' was defined by St. Thomas Aquinas as 'a vice opposed to religion by way of excess; not because in the worship of God it does more than true religion, but because it offers Divine worship to beings other than God or offers worship to God in an improper manner.' [2]

According to Catholic theologians, there are four species of superstitions: (1) improper worship of the true God; (2) idolatry; (3) divination; and (4) vain observances, which include magic and occult arts. The origin of superstition is, in the first place, subjective. Ignorance of natural causes may lead to the belief that certain striking phenomena express the will or the anger of some invisible overriding power, and the objects in which such phenomena appear are forthwith deified, e.g. in Nature-worship. On the other hand many superstitious practices are due to a false interpretation or an exaggerated notion of natural events. There were plenty of superstitions among the Jews, and the writer of The Book of Wisdom remarks:

'What folly it argues in man's nature, this ignorance of God! So much good seen, and he, who is existent Good, not known! Should they not learn to recognize the Artificer by the contemplation of his works? Instead, they have pointed us to fire, or wind, or to the nimble air, wheeling stars, or tempestuous waves, or sun and moon, and made gods of them to rule the world! Perhaps the beauty of such things bewitched them into mistaking it for divinity? Ay, but what of him who is Master of them all; what excellence must be his, the Author of all beauty, that could make them! Or was it power, and power's exercise, that awoke their wonderment? Why then, how many times greater must he be, who contrived it! Such great beauty even creatures have, reason is well able to contemplate the Source from which these perfections came.

'Yet, if we find fault with men like these, their fault is little by comparison; err they may, but their desire is to find God, and it is in that search they err. They stop short in their enquiry at the contemplation of his creatures, trusting only in their senses, that find such beauty there. Excuse them, then, we may not; if their thoughts could reach far enough to form a judgment about the world around them, how is it they found, on the way, no trace of him who is Master of it? But there are men more wretched yet, men who repose all their confidence in

[2] *Summa Theologica*, II–II, Q. xcii, a.1.

a world of shadows. They give the name of god to what is made by human art, gold and silver that human workmanship has turned into the likeness of living things, blocks of senseless stone that human hands have carved, long ago.' [3]

Like many another Jew, the fishermen apostles were superstitious, as fishermen have always been during the past nineteen hundred years. For it is related that when they saw a mysterious figure moving over the top of the waves towards their storm-tossed boat, terror seized them. They took it for granted that it was a ghost, possibly the earth-bound spirit of a man who had been drowned on the Sea of Galilee.[4] It never occurred to the crew that this 'apparition' was their master, Jesus.

Witchcraft, i.e. the malevolent exercise of preternatural powers, especially by women, attributed to a connection with the Devil or demons, is mentioned in several books of the Old Testament.[5] Tertullian, St. Augustine, and other Early Christian writers believed in the existence of witchcraft; although there were others of the Fathers, e.g. St. Hippolytus, St. John Chrysostom and St. Caesarius of Arles who were opposed to the belief. On the whole during the early Middle Ages, bishops tried to stop the persecution of witches. Gregory VII, who was Pope from 1073 to 1085, forbade the killing of women for supposed crimes such as causing storms and epidemics, but Popes Alexander IV (1258), and later John XXII (1320) gave permission to the Inquisition to deal with cases of witchcraft if connected with heresy.[6] In 1484 Innocent VIII urged the Inquisition to be ruthless against witches, when reports came of their intercourse with Satan, transformations into animals, and evil spells cast over human beings and cattle. As will be related in this book, the sixteenth century Reformers, with their often exaggerated belief in the power of the devil, were tireless in hunting down alleged witches and warlocks, usually burning them alive. In spite of the conclusions of the Jesuit Frederic Spee, published in *Cautio Criminalis circa Processus contra Sagas* (1631), that many so-called witches in Germany were entirely innocent, and that they ought to be treated with more caution and circumspection, numerous writers all through the seventeenth century, both Catho-

---

[3] 13:1–10 (Knox version).
[4] cf. Matthew 14:22–32; Mark 6:45–52; John 6:15–21.
[5] e.g. 1 Samuel 28:7–25; Exodus 22:18; and Deuteronomy 18:10.
[6] The Inquisition, so called, had been established by Gregory IX about 1232. He feared the decree passed by the Emperor Frederick II entrusting the hunting out of heretics to state officials, and so claimed this office for the Church, and appointed papal inquisitors.

lics and Protestants, defended the death penalty for sorcerers. The last trials for witchcraft in England took place in 1712, in Scotland in 1727, in Switzerland in 1782 and in Germany in 1793. Since then witches and other persons engaging in white and black magic have been left alone in all European countries, unless they have become a public nuisance.

It was about forty-five years ago that I began to be interested in old fisher customs, taboos and superstitions. Since then I have gone on collecting stories about them, particularly in France and on the East Coast of Scotland. I first became aware of what St. Thomas Aquinas defined as 'a vice opposed to religion by way of excess' in 1920, when I spent a week at sea in a Brixham sailing trawler. Two trips to the Dogger Bank in a Grimsby steam-trawler initiated me into more taboos and superstitions. The greater part of the summer of 1921 was spent ashore and afloat with fishermen on the Moray Firth Coast of Scotland. I soon realized that there were all sorts of things which could not be done, or words that could not be used for fear of bad luck. For instance, I was told that I must never ask a fisherman where he intended to shoot his lines or nets if I met him on his way to the harbour. It was difficult to memorize the persons, animals and names all capable, so it was alleged, of exercising evil influences. Priests, ministers, pigs, hares, foxes and rabbits could not be mentioned, but the most dangerous word was salmon.

One day I was standing with the skipper's son in the wheel-house of the Buckie steam-drifter, *Monarch*, or her way up Loch Ness, bound for the herring fisheries off the Outer Hebrides. Knowing that I had often stayed with the Benedictine monks at Fort Augustus Abbey, 'Jeems' asked if I had ever done any fishing on the Loch. Without thinking I replied: 'Oh yes, plenty of . . .' But before I had time to utter the fatal word 'salmon,' he had pushed his hand in front of my mouth. 'Na, na!' he remarked nervously, 'ye dinna say yon word; I ken fine fat ye mean!'

My instruction continued for the next two months. More than one elderly fisherman confided to me that he believed in the powers for good and evil held by 'wise-women,' i.e. witches. Hints were conveyed of the existence of fairies and sea-devils. Living among fisher folk on the North East Coast of Scotland, so I soon realized, involved much forethought and tact. It was so easy to do the wrong thing, or to refer to the wrong persons or animals. Taken all round, the rules and observances of this close-knit maritime community, composed mainly of Presbyterians, were more elaborate than those of the Benedictine monks with whom I had lived for the past eleven years. But they were not written down, and one had to rely on oral instruction. There were no printed Constitutions to consult!

In some ways it was easier to become intimate with fishermen on the coast of Normandy, because the majority were practising, even if not always pious, Catholics. During the first two months of 1922 I made many friends at Port-en-Bessin and Fécamp. In a sense these men and lads were more open than those with whom I had been associating on the North East Coast of Scotland. They were quite ready to answer my questions about old customs, taboos and superstitions. Later on came opportunities to study those of Italian fishermen. In a more superficial manner for inability to talk to them in their own language, I began to investigate the folk-lore of Danish and German seafarers. The greater part of the summer of 1930 was spent on the coasts of Brittany, where I visited almost every fishing port and all the larger islands. Here I found a wealth of maritime superstitions, which were a mixture of paganism and Catholicism.

From 1938 to 1958 my home was beside Macduff harbour, a busy fishing port in Banffshire, where it was easy to add to my knowledge of old customs, because all my neighbours were fisher folk. Now I am living in a back-of-beyond, end-of-the-road moribund fisher community on the coast of Angus, where maritime folk-lore is not altogether forgotten. This book has been written in a two-roomed cottage which has been occupied by sea-faring families since my maternal great-grandfather granted the original feu-charter to David Coull, fisherman, in 1841. The frontispiece depicts two fishermen neighbours baiting their lines beneath my roof, for occasionally they revert to this the most ancient method of catching fish as a change from a seine net.[7] Some of their gear is stored alongside my books.

When I first began to be interested in fisher folk-lore, the capture of fish still depended to a great extent on the moods of the winds and the waves, although steam had long since superseded sail in all larger ports. Life both ashore and afloat was still surrounded by fears and forebodings. There were as yet no daily weather reports on the radio; no scientific devices to make it easier to

---

[7] The parable of the 'net that was cast into the sea, and enclosed fish of every kind at once' (Matthew 13:47) is repeated daily in countless fishing ports around our coasts, and often in a more convincing manner than when it was addressed by our Lord to his hearers by the Sea of Galilee. The Danish seine net (*Snurrevaed*), which rapidly superseded long and hand-lines in most Scottish fishing districts after the first World War, is merely a modern version of the Galilean net, involving less physical labour.

capture fish, or for a vessel to find her position at sea, except by
means of a compass. There was still mystery on every side. Yet
diesel engines, radio-telephones, echo-meters, and many more
gadgets have not managed to drive away mystery altogether. There
is no doubt that old traditions die hard, and that folk-lore is still
a living force among Scots fishermen, even if the younger men
are often ashamed to admit it.

I realize this from time to time, for instance, when I have been
chatting with any of *Rosemary's* crew around my fireside on a
winter night. I retire to bed, and listen to the distant roar of the
waves, and the soughing of the wind. It is not so very difficult to
believe that witches, kelpies and other ghostly apparitions might
be encountered were I to wander along the cliffs towards Scurdy-
ness Lighthouse.

With no conscious effort fisher taboos and superstitions have
been absorbed into my system during the past forty-five years. Even
to-day at the age of seventy-five nothing would induce me to throw
fish bones on the fire. I am glad that the position of my bed makes
it impossible for the moon to shine on my face, because I have
not forgotten that this might easily land me up in the nearest
mental hospital! There are many more superstitions which are
recorded in one or other chapter of this book which I find myself
obeying instinctively. In conclusion, it is worth stating that most
of the stories here told of Scottish taboos and superstitions were
confirmed by an octogenarian fisherman at Portsoy, Banffshire.

PETER F. ANSON
July 25th, 1964
Feast of St. James the Greater,
fisherman on the Sea of Galilee

Ferryden,
Montrose,
Angus

CONTENTS

CONTENTS

Chapter One

THE FISHERMAN'S HOME—THE SOCIAL BACKGROUND OF FISHER FOLK

IN order to understand fisher folk-lore it is essential to have an idea of how fishermen and their families lived both ashore and afloat during the centuries when most of the old traditional customs, taboos and superstitions recorded in this book were widespread. Fisher folk have always formed communities of their own; more conservative usually than agricultural or industrial workers. They were and still are closely knit together.

Writing about a hundred years ago, Mr. James Bertram said:

'I have a considerable acquaintance with the fisher-folk; and while engaged in collecting information about the fisheries, and in investigating the natural history of the herring and other food-fishes, have visited most of the Scottish fishing villages and many of the English ones, nor have I neglected Normandy, Brittany and Picardy; and wherever I went I found the fisher-folk to be the same, no matter whether they talked a French *patois* or a Scottish dialect, such as one may hear at Buckie on the Moray Firth, or in the *Rue de Pollet* of Dieppe. The manners, customs, mode of life, and even the dress and superstitions, are nearly the same on the coast of France as they are on the coast of Fife. . . .' [1]

This is just as true to-day, perhaps more so, because the fishing industry has now become highly standardized, just as have ways of living. National and even local distinctions are far less noticeable.

To start with the fisherman's house: until fairly recent times it was always planned functionally in all parts of Northern Europe. No matter how simple were these houses, they were designed to suit the daily life of the men, women and children who occupied them. The actual design varied according to the district and the materials available. Houses were usually built as near as possible to the harbour or quays where the boats were berthed. As there were no bye-laws affecting town and village planning, the houses were often crowded together. No fisherman wanted to walk any distance from his house to his boat or vice versa, especially if he had heavy gear to carry backwards and forwards. Again, he had to keep an eye on his boat, especially in stormy weather.

[1] *The Harvest of the Sea* (2nd ed. 1869), p. 418.

On most parts of the North East Coast of Scotland early in the last century, the materials were stones and clay, stone and turf, or rounded water-worn stones, embedded in clay, mixed with chopped straw or heather. The inside walls were plastered with clay and whitewashed with lime. The roof timbers were usually covered with thatch, either or straw, heather or broom. Later on red tiles were substituted for thatch, and in some places the houses were given slate roofs. No house could be built without the workmen being offered whisky or ale, with bread and cheese, when the foundation stone was laid. The quasi-sacramental symbolism of whisky, bread and cheese will be mentioned again and again farther on.

The typical fisherman's house on the East Coast of Scotland early in the last century, when much building was done once the herring fisheries began to develop after the Napoleonic wars, and harbours were erected in many places where hitherto the boats had been tied up among the rocks, had but one door, opening into the kitchen. This room was open from floor to roof. The floor was earthen, and seldom level. The roof soon became black from the smoke of the peat fire. Strong boards were hung between some of the couples. From them were suspended dried fish, bunches of onions, a bunch or two of rush-pith for lamp-wicks, dried herbs for home-made medicines, a bunch of bent-grass ('bruckles') or sedge ('stars') to 'redd,' i.e. clean, clay tobacco pipes.[2] The earthen floor, usually kept well sanded, was a practical arrangement when lines were baited in the kitchen. The primitive lamp, known as the 'eely dolly,' remained the only form of illumination until well on in the nineteenth century when paraffin burning lamps came into use. Fishermen smoked plug tobacco, which needed much rolling and squeezing before it was pressed into a clay pipe, which was not regarded as properly seasoned until its bowl was stained dark brown with nicotine juice.

A tinder-box was the means to obtain a light. Lucifer matches were not on sale until after 1835. The tinder-box usually consisted of a cow's horn filled with charred linen. What was known as the 'flourish' was a small piece of steel, about two inches long, with a curved end. To obtain a light the cork stopper had to be removed from the horn, which was placed on the knees. Taking the flourish in one hand and the flint in the other, rubbing them together made sparks, which, falling on the dry tinder, caused the latter to

---

[2] On most parts of the East Coast of Scotland the older fisher-women used to smoke a 'clay cutty,' and also enjoyed chewing plug tobacco, just as the men did.

smoulder. Finally there was a flame. Long after lucifer matches came into general use about the middle of the last century, old fishermen preferred to light their pipes from a tinder-box. They said that the potassium chlorate paste on the match gave a nasty taste to the tobacco.

The same complicated process was involved when lighting a fire. On some parts of the North East Coast of Scotland it was the custom when moving from one house to another to carry along 'kindling,' i.e. burning peat, with which to start the fire in the new home. This was supposed to bring good luck, and it was a very old superstition.[3]

The kitchen fire-place in all working-class houses during the earlier decades of the last century was wholly open, and peat was the fuel. The hearth was raised a few inches above the earth floor. A 'crook' dangled over it from the 'rantle-tree.' Usually there was a 'bole' (niche) in the wall on either side of the hearth. The one contained a clay 'cutty' or two, a tobacco box, a candlestick ('can'le-gullie'), and sometimes a few books. The latter often included chap-books, the bawdy humour of which appealed to fishermen as well as country folk.[3a] The other niche generally held a wooden box, shaped like a house, with a round hole in the front, and known as the 'saat-backet.'

There was very little furniture, and it consisted, first, of the 'bench' on which were ranged plates, spoons and bowls. Under the 'bench' was the 'dresser,' with a row of wooden bowls and basins. Beneath it were stored pots, pans and pails. On the other side of the kitchen was a wooden 'settle' or 'dais,' with a table fixed to the wall, and folding down over it in the centre.

The chief feature of the typical fisher kitchen in almost every country of Northen Europe was the large box-bed, generally closed by a sliding or folding door. Some kitchens contained a second box-bed for the children. When the family increased two or three of the younger bairns often slept on the floor beneath their parents, or in ordinary wooden beds in another room. There was little or no privacy.

Fishing lines, hair for 'tippens' (hair that binds a hook to the line), hooks, 'fish-hakes' (frames for drying fish), and balls of strong twine, were never absent from a fisher kitchen. Space also had to be found for herring nets, buoys and even sails, where there were no sheds in which to store them.

[3] cf. J. M. McPherson, *Primitive Beliefs in the North-East of Scotland* (1929), p. 108.
[3a] See pp. 49–50.

B

There was not much light in the kitchen because the windows, never more than two, were very small. Sometimes they could not be opened. Fresh air was not wanted inside any fisherman's house. The family lived in a damp fug, composed of peat reek, wet clothes in winter when they could not be dried outside, and generally the smell of mussel bait.

The older houses seldom contained more than two rooms, and the second one was known as the 'but ein,' later 'ben-the-hoose.' Some houses, however, contained a 'middle-room' opening off the passage ('trance'), connecting the kitchen with the 'but ein.' The latter was usually furnished with a few chairs, a chest of drawers, a mirror, and one or two cupboards in the wall. The wooden bed was known as a 'bun breest.'

If anybody moved from one house to another, it was regarded as unlucky if the previous owner had thoroughly swept and cleaned it. Luck could also be taken away from a house by pulling a rope round it contrary to the course of the sun. If the new owners had suspicions that a spell had been cast on their home, they believed they could avert it by throwing in a cat before they entered the door.

From accounts of fishermen's houses on the East Coast of Scotland found in local histories, it is easy to picture what they were like in different places. Early in the last century the typical house at Cellardyke in Fife was little more than a narrow smoke-begrimed cot. The walls were rough and unplastered. The rafters of the low roof bore the marks of the joiner's axe. As elsewhere the floor of the kitchen or living room was bare earth, as uneven and damp as the path outside. Beside the open fire-place stood the 'creepie,' a sort of low stool which served as a chair. Beneath the little window, filled with coarse greenish glass, through which the sun hardly found its way, was a strong sea-chest holding clothes. The big double box-bed lay hidden away behind doors. A wooden press, a table, and a corner shelf with its array of dishes and ornaments, completed the furniture of this much used room. Outside in the yard were rough tarred sheds where nets and fishing gear were stored. Then, as now, a fisherman's house was never complete without its clothes lines, upon which washing always seemed to be 'bleaching' on fine days.[4]

About 1810 it was decided to build new houses for the fisher families in the Footdee district of Aberdeen. Plans were approved for two-storied houses, but both the men and women absolutely refused to live upstairs, and insisted that earthen floors were essen-

[4] cf. George Gourlay, *Memorials of Cellardyke* (Cupar, 1879).

tial for the kitchens, so the designs had to be changed. Mr. James Bertram visited Footdee in the late 1860s and wrote:

'The houses are peculiarly constructed. There are neither doors nor windows in the outside walls, although they look to all points of the compass; and none live within the square but the fishermen and their families, so that they are completely isolated and secluded from public gaze as a regiment of soldiers within the dead walls of a barrack. . . In the South Square only three of the houses are occupied by single families, and in the North Square only three, the others being occupied by at least two families each—one room apiece—and four *single* rooms in the North Square contain *two* families each! There are thirty-six married couples and nineteen widows in the twenty-eight houses; and the number of distinct families in them is fifty-four.' [5]

A local journalist wrote about the Footdee (commonly known as 'Fittie') fisher folk about the same time:

'They have the reputation of being a very peculiar people, and so in many respects they are; but they have also the reputation of being a dirtily-inclined and degraded people, and this we can certify from personal inspection that they are not. We have visited both squares, and found the interior of the houses as clean, sweet, and wholesome as could well be desired. Their white-washed walls and ceiling, their well-ribbed furniture, clean bedding, and freshly-sanded floors, present a picture of tidiness such as is seldom to be met with among classes of the population reckoned higher in the social scale. . . . Especially is this noticed in the care of their children, whose education might, in some cases, bring a tinge of shame to the cheek of well-to-do town's folk. Go down to the fisher squares, and lay hold of some little fellow hardly able to waddle about without assistance in his thick made-down moleskin,[6] and you will find he has the Shorter Catechism at his tongue-end. Ask any employer of labour in the neighbourhood of the shore where he gets his best apprentices, and he will tell you that for industry and integrity he finds no lads who surpass those from the fisher squares. Inquire about the families of the fishermen who have lost their lives while following their perilous occupation, and you will find that they have been divided among other families in the square, and treated by the heads of these families as affectionately as if they had been their own.' [7]

[5] *The Harvest of the Sea* (1869), pp. 449–50.
[6] Moleskin is a kind of shaggy cotton fustian with its surface shaved before dyeing, at one time much used for working men's trousers by reason of its good wearing qualities.   [7] ibid., pp. 451–2.

At Buckie on the Banffshire coast most of the fishermen's houses until after 1850 were single-storied, with two or three rooms, and a lean-to shed for nets. The newly built ones were roofed with slates, but the older still retained their turf thatch. In the smaller fishing villages it was the custom for the fisher folk to smoke haddocks over their peat fires for family use. They acquired a delicate yellow tinge, and tasted better than the article sold in shops.

Mr. Gregor recorded what life was like in a house such as has been described.[8] Over the peat fire hung a large iron pot. On a winter evening light was given by thin splinters of bog-fir, fixed in a sort of candlestick; also by an iron lamp, known as the 'eely dolly.' The oil used was made from the livers of haddock, cod, ling and other fish, and was called 'black oil.' The wick consisted of the pith of rushes, although later on cotton thread was used.

The women were usually busy knitting some article of clothing. The men and lads might be found mending nets or making fishing lines. The younger children probably had less homework to keep them occupied. When this was finished they enjoyed singing songs, or listening to tales, especially those about fairies, witches, warlocks, and compacts with the Devil.

Contemporary with the typical fisherman's house on the East Coast of Scotland, which has been described, is Charles Dickens' account of Peggotty's house at Yarmouth found in *David Copperfield*. It was an up-turned black fishing vessel, high and dry on a dull waste of ground, with an iron funnel sticking out of the hull, and 'smoking very cosily.' There were probably other fisher homes like this one, whose owners 'dealt in lobsters, crabs and crawfish,' and who kept the pots and kettles 'in little wooden outhouses.' Dickens can hardly have invented 'the beautifully clean inside' of Peggotty's home, because it agrees with first-hand records of many other houses on the coast of East Anglia about the same date. This was probably not the only one with 'a table, a Dutch clock, and a chest of drawers, and on the chest of drawers a tea-tray with a painting of a lady with a parasol, taking a walk with a military looking child who was trailing a hoop.' Very common too at that date were 'coloured pictures, framed and glazed, of Scripture subjects,' also pictures of luggers. There were 'hooks in the beams of the ceiling besides 'lockers and boxes which served for seats and eked out the chairs.' Just as in Scotland, most fisher houses on the East Coast of England had box-beds; and it was in one of these that young David Copperfield slept; and listened to 'the winds

---

[8] op. cit., Chapter X, 'Evenings at the Fireside,' pp. 54–8.

getting up out at sea,' and knew that 'the fog was creeping up over the desolate flat outside.' [9]

By 1850 open boats had been superseded by decked boats almost all round the East Coast of Scotland. A higher standard of living accompanied a more comfortable way of life at sea, for most fishermen were better off financially. Writing in 1849, Mr. James Thomson said:

'That there is much comfort intermixed with a good deal of poverty in the larger Scottish fishing villages is evinced from the interior of the dwelling. In many a cottage, the "but end," as it is called, has everything of the best; there the eye is gratified by the most inviting of beds for the stranger, the mahogany chairs and chest of drawers, and all the other corresponding articles of furniture, betokening the rewards of thrift and industry. In the other or more common end, there is everything useful and necessary for the daily affairs of domestic life, whilst an array of Staffordshire ware stands on a bench opposite the fire-place, exhibiting the taste and fancy of the goodwife in a plenitude of variety, dazzling to the eye of the visitor and flattering to the vanity of the amiable possessor.' [10]

But the kitchen floor was still earth, and nets and creels, together with all the gear for baiting lines, helped to create a maritime atmosphere. In some houses the doors had already been taken away from the box-beds, and replaced by washable curtains and a pelmet of gay colours. In front of the bed was usually a large chest ('kist') containing the Sunday clothes of the men-folk, and which served as a seat. Wooden bowls and mugs had been superseded by china plates and cups.

The boats grew larger as the fishermen grew richer. 'Skaffies' were succeeded by 'Fifies,' and about 1880 the first 'Zulu' was launched. Many of these big sailing vessels used to fish for herring as far off as the south of Ireland, the Hebrides, the Shetlands, and the coast of East Anglia according to the season of the year. Sometimes, but not always, when the crew returned home in the late autumn they had money to burn, and much of it was spent on improving their houses. Invariably they brought back presents for their wives and children. So the mantelpieces were laden with stoneware figures, brilliantly coloured—sailors with their sweethearts, shepherdesses, and almost certain, Burns and Highland

[9] op. cit., Chapter III.
[10] *The Scottish Fisheries*, p. 181.

Mary, possibly Queen Victoria and her lamented husband the Prince Consort, together with one or two china dogs.

Most likely the 'end room' now contained a glass-fronted cupboard displaying the best tea set, only used on special occasions. The walls began to display framed paintings of fishing vessels, bought at Lowestoft or Yarmouth; also family photographs. Framed memorial cards of deceased relatives were another popular form of decoration. The rooms had long since been given ceilings, and in many houses the open peat fire had been superseded by an iron cooking range, burning coal. Very few houses had running water inside until fairly late in the century. Many had no sort of sanitary arrangements. The older fishermen were quite content to retire to an unobserved corner outside their houses or go on to the rocks when they had occasion to relieve nature. Nearly all their houses now had tarred wooden sheds adjacent to them, where nets and fishing gear were stored. New fishermen's houses on the East Coast of Scotland were almost invariably given large lofts or attics, for stowing herring nets, and where they were mended between the fishing seasons.

The same process of a gradual evolution from poverty to comparative affluence among the fisher folk took place in France and in other North European countries during the last century. In most French fisher communities, however, the houses were usually two-storied, although crowded together in just the same way as they were in Scottish towns and villages.

Yet there are some villages in Brittany where the fishermen's houses, generally built of grey granite, or white washed, are almost identical with the single-storied 'but-and-a-ben' which, until after the middle of the last century, was practically universal in Scotland.

Both French and Scots fishermen until fairly recent times took care to have amulets or charms in their kitchens. On the Côtes-du-Nord there were few families who did not have a statuette of the *Sainte Vierge,* often decorated with a bunch of dried seaweed or a laurel wreath. Elsewhere shells arranged in the shape of a cross were popular. In some villages the women used to recite what was known as *'la formulette de Sainte Barbe'* when the boats were at sea, kneeling before the image of our Lady or the hanging crucifix in the kitchen. It consisted of five Our Fathers and five Hail Marys. The favourite Scottish charm was a horse-shoe. A big 'buckie' shell (winkle) was sometimes hung above the hearth in stormy weather as an amulet. Shetland fishermen believed it would bring them good luck if the bones of a turbot were hidden somewhere in the house.

Nowhere else in northern Europe have so many old customs, taboos and superstitions survived than on the Ile-de-Sein, which will be mentioned again and again in this book. It lies off the Point-du-Raz, the most westerly headland in Brittany, about ten miles from Audierne, the nearest port. It consists of little more than the exposed portion of a reef of rocks, not more than a few yards above high-water mark, one-and-a-half miles long, and about half a mile broad. Until recent times the inhabitants, roughly 1,000, remained untouched by the advance of modern civilization. Fishing has always been the chief occupation. The village clusters around the church at the east end of the island. The little houses huddle close together, separated by narrow alleys. All the work on the land is done by the women. When they are ashore, the men fill in the time mending nets, or repairing lobster-pots and boats.

Every skipper's house on the Ile-de-Sein used to have suspended from the ceiling of its kitchen a boat made from the hollowed-out crust of a loaf of brown bread, sloop-rigged, with paper sails. Once a year, the Sunday before Lent, the skipper invited his crew to supper. This was known in Breton as the *Fest ar vag*, or boat feast. The men sat down to a meal consisting of soup, fresh meat and vegetables, followed by a cake made of wheat flour, prunes and eggs. A litre of wine was set before each man. The crew provided brandy. At the end of the meal all stood up, with their caps in their hands. The oldest member of the crew took down the boat. Then the skipper made the sign of the cross, broke the bread of which the boat was made, and divided it up among the crew. This was regarded as a sacramental rite, binding them together, body and soul. One of the men took a new loaf lying on the table, hollowed out the crust, and rigged a boat like the old one which had been dismantled. This done, the crew saluted the vessel three times while reciting the *Veni Creator*. So ended the annual *Fest ar vag*, after grace had been said. But on the first Friday in Lent there was another ceremonial repast consisting of fish and potatoes, provided by the crew. After it was over the *mousse*, or cabin-boy, distributed what remained of the brandy to widows and poor relations.

At Plouer, a small village on the Côtes-du-Nord, between Saint-Brieuc and Paimpol, it used to be the custom before the fishing fleet left for the Newfoundland Banks or Iceland to hang a leek from one of the joists of the kitchen ceiling. If the plant kept alive, this was regarded as a good omen, but if it dried up and died, then it could be taken as certain that a member of the family had perished at sea.[11]

[11] cf. Sébillot, *Le Folk-Lore des Pêcheurs* (1901), p. 76.

There were certain actions which had to be avoided in any fisherman's house. In Scottish fisher communities it was regarded as unlucky to offer a light to another man to light his pipe; but if it was impossible not to render this service, then the moment that he went out of the door a handful of salt had to be thrown on the fire.[12] To counteract evil influences of other kinds, e.g. when milk boiled over the edge of a pot and ran into the fire, salt had to be thrown into it.[13]

In olden times there existed innumerable superstitions connected with the manner of eating fish. On the coast of Cornwall, for instance, it was regarded as unlucky to start with the head; if one began with the tail, there would be good fishing.[14] On the East Coast of Scotland no family dared to burn the bones of fish or their shells. Haddock bones especially had to be treated with respect, for there was a legend that the black spots on its skin were the marks left by the finger and thumb of St. Peter when he opened the fish's mouth and took out the piece of silver to pay the tax in the temple: a haddock is alleged to have said once:

> *Roast me an' boil me,*
> *But dinna burn ma beens,*
> *Or than I'll be a stranger*
> *Aboot yir hearth steens.*

Another version of this rhyme ran:

> *Roast me weel, or boil me weel,*
> *But dinna burn ma beens,*
> *An' ye'll get plenty o' fish*
> *Aboot yir fire steens.*

Skate was a fish believed to have various effects when eaten. It was regarded as an aphrodisiac.[14a] The water in which skate was boiled —'skate-bree'—was said to be a certain cure for rheumatism. It was a fairly common custom on the North East Coast of Scotland until recent times for fishermen to keep back skate caught, dry them in the sun, cut their names on the hard skin, and take them home. In 1960 an aged fisherman at Portsoy, Banffshire, told the author that he had kept a dried skate in his house for twenty years, and

---

[12] W. Gregor, in *Folk-Lore Journal*, Vol. IV, p. 309.
[13] W. Gregor, *Notes on the Folk-Lore of the North-East of Scotland*, p. 193.
[14] cf. W. Hunt, *Popular Romances of Cornwall*, p. 368.
[14a] See pp. 55, 64.

then presented it to a newly married couple, convinced that it would help them to breed a large family.

Taken all round, life in a typical fisher family a hundred years ago was not easy because there were so many things which could not be done for fear of bad luck. Every day of the week had some superstition connected with it. Monday was an unlucky day on which to start any kind of work; it had to be postponed until Tuesday. Friday was even more dangerous. Saturday was safe enough, on the other hand, a new moon on Saturday was almost certain to bring bad weather. The months of the year could not be disregarded; some were lucky, others were not. It was most unlucky to see the new moon for the first time through a window, or with empty hands. On the first sight of a new moon, a wise fisherman took care to turn any money he had in his trouser pockets. Most seamen regarded it as dangerous to sleep with the moon shining on the face, for it might well cause madness; if not, then the whole or partial paralysis of the face. It was unlucky to sing before breakfast, and there was an old warning:

> '*Sing afore breakfast,*
> *Greet aifter it.*'

The surest way to break off a friendship was to make a present of a knife, a pair of scissors, or any sharp pointed instrument. After hair had been cut, the bits had to be burned and never thrown out. To charge a person with theft was sure to end in disaster. If anybody returned an object which had been stolen, it was safer to let him keep it. 'Nae stoun faangs i' the hoose' was a sound maxim to remember.

A stranger would have made endless mistakes without realizing it, to the horror of the more superstitious members of the household. To stir food from right to left, instead of from left to right, was sure to result in stomach aches, even bowel diseases. When dressing, the right stocking had to be put on first, also the right shoe or boot. If one dared to sew on a button, or even a single stitch, on Sunday, one could be sure that the Devil would undo the work at night. When any man donned a new pair of trousers he put a coin, known as a 'hansel,' in one of the pockets. A kiss was given and taken from the wearer of a new dress. When a boy or girl, wearing new clothes, entered a neighbour's house, they were given something as 'hansel.' Men and boys always tried to keep a crooked sixpence in their pockets for good luck. These are but a few of the superstitions connected with everyday life.[15]

[15] Most of those recorded here have been taken from either William

The clothes worn by fisher folk in most countries were associated to a certain degree with superstitions. There was a feeling, not always clearly defined, that they lost their efficacy to withstand the forces of evil if they did not conform to traditional patterns, handed down for generations. For as Thomas Carlyle wrote in *Sartor Resartus*: 'Clothes have made men of us; hence the beginnings of wisdom is to look fixedly on clothes . . . till they become transparent. . . . Clothes are the accidental standards of multitudes more or less sacredly uniting together; in which union itself, there is something mystical and borrowing from the God-like. . . . It is in and through symbols that man, consciously and unconsciously, lives, works and has his being; those ages, moreover, are accounted the noblest which can best recognize symbolic worth, and prize it at the highest.'

Fisher folk are not the only social class by any means who until living memory accepted Carlyle's belief in the symbolic value of clothes. Romanies (who usually prefer to be called 'travellers' than gipsies) retained distinctive styles of dress, which were bound up with their folk-lore, until they were driven to give up horse-drawn wagons for motor-trailers. Dominic Reeve, a life-long traveller, tells us:

> 'A real old-style traveller with any pride in himself and his possessions would always be very particular about the fashions and cut of his clothes. The suits always followed very special designs, incorporating certain features such as yokes to the coats, raised seams, scalloped flaps to all pockets; whilst the trousers used to be made with leg-of-mutton shaped legs, stitched bottoms, raised seams, and a "flap" or "fall" front in place of the contemporary "fly." These suits were generally made in the old days, in very heavy cloths, such as Derby tweed, covert cloth, Melton, cavalry twill, Bedford cord, or sometimes "moleskin."' [16]

As will be explained farther on, some of the 'special designs' mentioned by Dominic Reeve were incorporated in the clothes worn by fishermen, not only in England but in other north European countries, until nearly the close of the last century, just because

Henderson's *Notes on the Folk-Lore of the Northern Counties* (1879); Walter Gregor's *The Folk-Lore of the North-East of Scotland* (1881); or J. M. McPherson's *Primitive Beliefs in the North-East of Scotland* (1929). In many cases the stories given in these books have been confirmed or amplified by old fisher folk.

[16] *Whichever Way we Turn* (1964), p. 38.

they were regarded as symbolic standards of multitudes united together in the same calling.

Since it was the women who ruled over most fisher families it may be as well to give the details of their costumes before dealing with male clothes. In Brittany every large parish once had its own fashion (*kiz*) in female dress. They were divided into about twelve regions, each of which had its distinctive details. There was such a diversity in the shape of the *coiffes* worn by both the country women and those on the coast, that it would take up too much space to describe them even briefly.

On the coast of Normandy there used to be an almost equally great diversity in the clothes worn by the women, but the linen *coiffes* began to give way to bonnets sooner than in Brittany, and were worn only at local festivals. Moving northwards every fisher community in the Pas-de-Calais, and thence along the coasts of Flanders, Holland, Germany, Denmark, Sweden and Norway, retained its own slightly different fashions. The result was that in a crowd, it was fairly easy to tell from which locality a fishwife came.

Most fishing districts in England also had their own distinctive fashions in female dress. At Staithes in Yorkshire about 1890 the fishermen's wives and daughters usually wore lilac print aprons and sunbonnets, but if they were in mourning the colour was black. Their overskirts were turned up over red petticoats. Down the back the pinned-up drapery hung in folds. Over their shoulders a little plaid shawl was drawn. Arms were left bare to the elbow. At Stiffkey, on the coast of Norfolk, just as in many places on the North Coast of France, it was a common sight to find the women, with their skirts tucked high up above their knees, and barefooted, gathering cockles on the wet sands.

For more than a hundred years, and until after the Second World War, thousands of women and girls, drawn from all parts of Scotland and even Ireland, found employment gutting, salting and packing herring in ports as far distant from each other as Lerwick in Shetland and Lowestoft in Suffolk. Their working clothes consisted of long waterproof aprons, leather seaboots well up over the knee, shawls pinned on their shoulders over woollen jerseys, their hair protected by handkerchiefs fastened down over their heads. Their fingers were rolled round with bits of rag to prevent them being cut or pierced by herring bones. But to-day this form of female labour has almost disappeared.

The fishermen spoke different languages or dialects, but just because their jobs were more or less identical, also their manners, customs and even superstitions, they wore clothes which distinguished them from landsmen and which were the outward mark of their profession. Although each country, district, town or village had its own favourite materials and differences of cut, the costume was basically the same on every coast.

During the eighteenth century many fishermen, like sailors in the mercantile marine and the navy, often wore white petticoat-breeches. Double-breasted jackets of blue cloth predominated, also breeches and waistcoats of the same material. Black silk handkerchiefs were sometimes worn round the neck. In some fishing ports, petticoats continued to be the rule until about the eighteen-twenties. Red woollen knitted caps were popular. Coarse white linen or canvas trousers and jumpers were often worn at sea.

Charles Dickens—recalling Great Yarmouth as he first knew it about 1820—describes the young fisherman, Ham, as 'a huge strong fellow of six feet high, broad in proportion, and round-shouldered; but with a simpering boy's face and curly light hair that gave him quite a sheepish look. He was dressed in a canvas jacket, and a pair of such very stiff trousers that they would have stood quite as well alone, without any legs in them. And you couldn't so properly have said he wore a hat, as that he was covered in a-top, like an old building, with something pitchy.' [17] Paintings and engravings of early nineteenth century date show fishermen in stiff canvas trousers in other ports besides Yarmouth.

In E. W. Cooke's *Shipping and Craft,* published in 1829, several of the plates show fishermen and fishing boats at Brighton. Some of the fishermen are wearing hard hats, long coats, floppy leather sea-boots, and petticoats. Their hands are shoved into the deep pockets of these maritime kilts, which were popular on some parts of the coast of England until about the middle of the last century.

On the Thames Estuary about 1820 the working clothes of the shrimp fishermen at Leigh-on-Sea usually consisted of a flannel shirt, woollen drawers, reddish-brown pilot-cloth or kersey whole-fall trousers, with blue or white jerseys. During the summer months some men wore grey tweed trousers. Over their home-knitted jerseys they put on white calico jumpers. Mufflers (of various colours) were donned at sea. When working their nets, the men wore loose petticoat, oilskin trousers and a smock. their hands kept warm by thick woollen mittens. The universal short clay pipe completed the rig.

Throughout the eighteenth century, men of all classes of society in almost every part of Europe wore breeches made with a 'flap'

[17] *David Copperfield,* Chapter III.

or 'fall' front. Later on, when trousers eventually superseded breeches, this feature was retained by the 'lower orders' after the 'gentry,' taken as a whole, had adopted a 'fly,' with either side or cross pockets. Seafarers, almost without exception, from the Baltic to the Bay of Biscay, remained faithful to fall-front trousers. So too did agricultural labourers, navvies, gipsies, and even railway porters. Until the close of the last century no fisherman in any North European country wore anything else. Then a few young men began to have their trousers made with a 'fly' and cross pockets, but the new fashion spread slowly. Even to-day flap-fronted trousers are still worn by fishermen on parts of the coast of Normandy, and in a few places in the south of England, where the type of boats has remained more or less unchanged, except for the installation of motors.[18]

Practically every fisherman on the East Coast of Scotland a hundred years ago wore loose-fitting dark blue cloth or canvas whole-fall trousers. Before going to sea tapes were tied round the knees, and thick woollen stockings, reaching well above the knees, drawn over them. The leather sea-boots were made to measure, and reached to the top of the thigh. The leather, kept well-oiled, moulded itself to a man's leg, and was impervious to water. On shore the boots were often replaced by slippers. A black or brightly coloured silk handkerchief tied twice round the neck was as popular with fishermen as it was with gipsies until living memory. A hand-knitted jersey and a blue 'bonnet' with a tassel ('toorie'), shaped like a tam-o'-shanter, completed the working rig. Earlier in the century either a very tall or flattish silk hat, worn with a tilt at the back, and known as a 'rakie-step' was the correct headgear ashore for a skipper. Later on the blue 'bonnet' gave way in some places to a peaked 'cheese-cutter' cap, or a seal-skin cap. Navy blue serge or cloth suits, with bell-bottomed trousers and a double-breasted jacket, were worn by young fishermen on Saturday nights and Sundays.

There were some ports where the fisher lads during the earlier years of the last century displayed themselves in much more striking clothes on Sundays. At Leigh-on-Sea, Essex, for instance, they appeared in well-washed flap-fronted white duck trousers, sometimes with fringed bell-bottoms; the effect of which was enhanced by zebra-striped smocks, on which each lad had his full name embroidered on the front. His spectacular week-end 'rig'

[18] Whole-fall trousers remained a feature of the dress of men in the Royal Navy until 1956, when a zip-fastened 'fly,' also side and hip pockets, became part of the new uniform.

was completed by a jaunty red jersey-cap, white cotton stockings and slippers tied with ribbon. On other occasions the fisher lads wore well polished Blucher or Wellington boots imported from Rotterdam, via Harwich. On weekdays a clean white linen smock hid most of the blue jersey and showed off the plum-coloured pilot-cloth bell-bottomed trousers. The hair was worn long and kept well-curled.

On the Isle of Jersey, where old fisher customs lingered on much later than in most districts, even as late as the eighteen-nineties, every fisher lad when he was ashore wore very wide whole-fall bell-bottomed trousers, a blue pilot-cloth jacket with a blue velvet collar, and a silk muffler round his neck. His costume was finished off by a cheese-cutter cap, trimmed with black braid, and protected by a silk cover. When they were at sea the Jersey crews wore thick twilled cotton trousers with the traditional flap—*pantalon à pont* as the garment was called. Their blue jerseys sometimes had a shield knitted in front. White canvas smocks were often worn to save them from getting soiled. A bowler hat was the alternative to a cheese-cutter cap; a wide-brimmed felt hat the correct headgear at funerals, just as was a bowler in Scottish fishing villages, though the same sort of wide-brimmed felt hat was often worn. Incidentally, most fishermen in olden times had their name embroidered on all their garments, so that if they were drowned, it would be easy to identify their bodies.

Although separated by between three and four hundred miles of open sea, fishermen in Denmark had working clothes almost identical with those worn on the East Coasts of England and Scotland during the last century. A painting by M. Rörbye, who was practising his arts in the 1820s, records fishermen at Skagen wearing top-hats and loose petticoats, like those depicted by English artists about the same date. Paintings by Michael Ancher show Danish fishermen between 1880 and 1890 whose clothes hardly differ from those worn by fishermen on the other side of the North Sea. Most of the older men have a fringe of hair around their cheeks and chins, just as was the fashion at, e.g., Lowestoft and Yarmouth at this period. Others are bearded, and a few of the younger ones are clean shaven. Anna Ancher's paintings of fish-wives at Skagen might almost have been done on the East Coast of Scotland during the 1880s. Old photographs of Danish fishermen taken about seventy years ago show that their fashions in headgear were similar to those in many a port on the North Sea Coasts of England and Scotland. They even smoked the same shape of clay pipe.

During the second half of the last century, fishermen on many parts of the East Coast of Scotland used to have made to measure a double-breasted navy blue kersey sleeved-waistcoat, known as a 'byler.' It was usually lined with blue flannel. With loose fitting trousers of the same heavy material, it formed what was known as a 'byler suit.' [19]

The Scottish jerseys were home-knitted and tight fitting, much smarter than the long loose-fitting guernseys worn by most English fishermen. The neck was fastened at the left side by three or more buttons. An expert knitter decorated the whole or the upper part of the back, front and shoulders with elaborate patterns. Almost every fishing district in Britain had its own type of jersey, so by looking at a man, it was generally easy to know where he came from.

It was not only by the shape or patterns of a jersey that one could be fairly sure from what part of England or Scotland a fisherman belonged; even trousers had their local distinctions. In some communities the flap was square shaped; in others the sides were slightly rounded off. One locality favoured fairly tight trousers, another had them made loose. The crews of the fishing boats and sailing barges on the Medway and Lower Thames stuck to old fashions until well on in the present century. When they were ashore they liked to display themselves in double-breasted jackets, and short double-breasted waistcoats, over their blue jerseys, like those shown in some of Michael Ancher's paintings of Danish fishermen. Their whole-fall trousers were often widely splayed at the bottom—even with a slit in some cases, so that they draped over the boots. Although the usual material was navy blue pilot-cloth or serge, bell-bottomed trousers of a rose-tinted blue were also worn. Many men still had thin gold ear-rings, and almost all still smoked clay pipes.

It was not difficult to distinguish a Breton from a Norman fisherman when he was in his working clothes. The general effect of the former was sloppy. The men usually wore much patched blue jumpers and trousers, with black or blue berets. A grey or black woollen jersey showed up above the neck of the jumper. Later on red, pink or orange coloured jumpers and trousers added to the picturesqueness of many a fishing port in Brittany.

Except for small details the working clothes of a fisherman on the coast of Normandy were almost identical with those worn on the South Coast of England until living memory. White or reddish

[19] The old-style fisherman's waistcoat was reminiscent of the longer high-necked garment with round collar worn by 'travellers,' though the material was generally corduroy instead of heavy blue cloth.

brown linen or canvas jumpers, with a deep V-shaped opening, protected blue jerseys. Fall-front trousers of the same materials were almost universal. But instead of boots the men and boys invariably wore wooden sabots when they were ashore. The fishermen at Boulogne and in the small communities in Picardy could be distinguished from their brothers in Normandy by slight details in dress; and so it was when one got to the coast of Flanders.

The average fisherman's wife knitted thick woollen vests and drawers for the male members of her family, and made their flannel shirts. She also knitted long woollen stockings worn inside the leather sea-boots. Oilskin trousers, sou'westers and oilskin coats varied in design according to the country or district, but the colour was usually yellow.

Robert C. Leslie, the marine artist, described the oilskin garments worn by the fishermen-boatmen at Deal in his *Sea-Painter's Log*, published in 1886. He wrote:

'It was wonderful to watch the crew get into their sea-going "togs." Their outer oilskins rest on a foundation of thick pilot-cloth jackets, trousers and waistcoat without sleeves, while round the neck a woollen comforter three or four yards long was wound in this wise: a comrade would hold one end of the comforter, while the wearer, taking half a dozen turns, capstan-like, upon his axis, wound it about his neck. Then the wide oilskin trousers, reaching high up, were tied round the chest just under the arms and, over all, the long oilskin coat was tied from top to bottom; buttons are seldom used. A snug sou'wester, leaving little of the face exposed but the eyes and nose, completed the costume; and a more helpless-looking bundle than the boatman was when so encased it would be hard to picture. But those men knew their work; and though hardly able to move on land, yet as soon as they were afloat in the lugger all was done well and to the moment. . . .' [20]

A fisher lad's 'baptism' or 'brothering' was not complete until he had been clothed in the traditional garments of his profession.[21] From that moment his mother had to make sure that he was dressed exactly the same as his father or elder brothers. Not only had he to wear the correct garments, but he had to wear them in the right way. For instance, when he was not using his arms for any job, they had to be shoved into the flaps of his trousers, and not allowed

[20] op. cit., pp. 144–5.
[21] For these ceremonies, see pp. 50–3.

to dangle. The side buttons must never be done up.[22] Old photographs taken in the 1880s indicate that some Scottish fishermen
had no side buttons on their whole-fall trousers, only two centre
ones. When putting on a jersey the fisher lad had to be sure that it
was not on back to front, and pulled well down. Jackets were not
worn inside the house, above all when sitting down to a meal, but
caps could be left on.

It was not until about the end of the last century that fishermen
in the more primitive communities started to shave. Until then it
was rare to find one without a beard, especially on the East Coast
of Scotland.

It was the same on the East Coast of England, where full beards
remained fashionable with fishermen and fisher lads until the 1880s,
as can be seen in photographs of Edward Fitzgerald's good-looking
bearded fisherman friend at Lowestoft—'Posh' Fletcher—taken
about 1867. Later on most of the Lowestoft men, as well as those
on other parts of the North Sea coasts, retained only a narrow
fringe of hair below the cheeks and chin; the rest of the face being
shaved, probably once a week. This fashion survived at Lowestoft
among the older fishermen until about the First World War. They
also stuck to their white or tanned jumpers, sealskin caps, or high-
crowned hats and bowlers when they were ashore, if they did not
wear dark blue cloth cheese-cutter caps. It is interesting to note
that as long as sail persisted, almost every fisherman, young and old,
retained his heavy pilot-cloth blue or dark brown fall-front
trousers.

Thin gold ear-rings had been worn by seamen from the sixteenth
century. Very often a boy had his ears pierced soon after he went
to sea. These gold circles were not worn for ornament but as
amulets. The belief was that they would protect the wearers from
drowning, preserve the eye-sight, and cure rheumatism. In Catholic
countries a seaman or fisherman often wore a blessed medal or
two round his neck, or even a small scapular. Screwed on ear-
rings were not supposed to have the same magic powers as those
which pierced the lobes of the ears.[23]

Tattoo marks on the body were never regarded as so important

---

[22] The Romanies, the 'travellers' in England, before they abandoned their
horse wagons and old-style fashions in clothes, also left open the sides of
their fall-front trousers, which, unlike those worn by fishermen, were
narrow-legged, with stitched turn-ups.

[23] A belief in the magic qualities of blessed medals has survived among
French fishermen in some places where they have long since given up all
practice of religion. At Dieppe a few years ago many men and lads would
not go to sea without a collection of them.

C

by fishermen as by other classes of seamen; although those who had served in the mercantile marine or the naval reserves of their respective countries often had their arms or bodies tattooed with sacred or profane emblems, according to their fancy, and for superstitious reasons.

In the 'eighties of the last century the narrow paved streets of Lerwick in the Shetland Isles afforded infinite opportunities for studying fisher fashions in dress any Saturday night. It is recorded that:

'a quaintly picturesque mob are the Dutch fishermen, utterly unlike in many ways one's preconceived notions. Here they come some four or five, linked arm in arm, laughing and jabbering away. . . . Here is one big-built, fair-haired Frieslander in a magenta jersey, with petticoat trousers and blue stockings; here a little dark-eyed, spare man who looks Belgic, with a blue guernsey, canvas breeches and scarlet hose; here a third, ringing another variation on the colours of the rainbow. All have the curly-toed wooden shoes, and as they go, clatter, clatter, jabber, jabber, spreading around them an atmosphere of good humour and good temper. . . . There is also the little ten-year-old Dutch "man" dressed in a long coat reaching nearly down to his heels, with metal buttons and flapped side pockets, that fit him perfectly; a long-waisted waistcoat, knee-breeches, black stockings and shoes, with a go-to-meeting hat on, smoking a cigar— smoking too, in a matter-of-fact way, that shows that he had not had his first weed the day before yesterday.' [24]

When it came to colour, the Portuguese sardine fishermen had no rivals in Europe. Their head-gear was a tam-o'-shanter shaped *barrete*, falling on one side, ending with a round black tuft. Their woollen shirts and trousers were usually multi-coloured with Scottish plaid-like patterns. The women's dress was equally picturesque and original.

So far as can be discovered, most fisher families, no matter to what country or district they belonged, were content with a simple and almost unvarying diet, until well after the middle of the last century. The food was home produced, and the cooking reflected national or regional traditions. On the East Coast of Scotland until about 1850 an average fisher family lived on home-baked oatcakes, milk, kail-broth, turnips, potatoes and fish. Tea was already drunk by the poorer classes, though it was expensive. Ale and whisky

[24] J. R. Tudor, *The Orkneys and Shetlands* (1883), p. 450.

cost much less, and as will be explained farther on, vast quantities of both were drunk.

There were no doubt many other villages on the East Coast of Scotland besides Ferryden, Angus, where a fisher family had only one good dinner during the week, and that was on Sunday. Andrew Douglas, who became the first schoolmaster at Ferryden about 1805, related that 'a bit of good "flesh" (as they called beef)' for broth, and often a foot or two, with a dumpling made with currants and raisins, usually made up the Sunday dinner.

In most English fisher communities the food tended to be more solid. Soups and broths were never popular as in Scotland and France. The average East Anglian fisherman early in the last century liked heavy food and plenty of it. Puddings were always eaten before the meat course, followed by a cup of tea. It is not surprising that many of the men suffered from indigestion.

Except in teetotal families, English fisher children drank beer from an early age. In Scotland babies used to be put to sleep by their mothers with one, two or three half wine-glasses of whisky, so a boy had acquired the taste for it long before he went to sea.

Every fishing village on the East Coast of Scotland had numerous ale-houses during the first half of the last century. At Ferryden, for instance, there were thirteen in the parish, which allowed one to every twenty-four families. Between 1830 and 1840 the local publicans usually sold about eight ankers of 'small beer' a week, and the usual amount of whisky sold was one gill to a bottle of beer.[25] Dr. Brewster, the parish minister, commented on these ale-houses:

> 'Their influence is most pernicious in every respect; and it is truly lamentable to perceive the insensibility so generally manifested by the more influential classes to the rapidly increasing evils among the lower classes of the community, which so obviously proceed from this fertile source of corruption.'

Nevertheless Andrew Douglas, the schoolmaster, laid in a large stock of spirits, alleged to be for medicinal purposes. He charged lower prices for a gill of whisky than the publicans, and soon every fisherman in Ferryden was patronizing him. The demand for cheap whisky was so persistent that the schoolmaster was obliged to get a fresh stock from Montrose twice a day. The wholesale merchant

[25] An anker was a liquid measure of about 4 gallons used originally by smugglers for convenience of carriage on horseback. Later on it became a standard measure of 8½ gallons, or a cask holding this quantity.

remarked to the carrier that the 'dominie' was surely emptying the casks into the estuary of the river. Andrew Douglas himself wrote many years later: 'But through time the tide of my business emptied itself. The other houses lowered their charges to get a share of the increased drinking, and to recover their old customers.' [26]

It has been said that inebriety is the staff of Scottish national life, and this was certainly applicable to most fisher communities early in the last century. As Henry Grey Graham reminds us: 'Drinking was the favourite vice of the country; it brought no shame, and it seemed to impair no constitution.' [27]

The poet Burns was expressing the opinion of many a Scots fisher lad when he wrote:

> '*Leeze me on drink; it gie's us mair*
> *Then either school or college.*'

Although he was thinking more of the country-side in his 'cantata' entitled *Love and Liberty*, the words could have been shouted by countless fishermen young and old from the Pentland Firth to Berwick-on-Tweed:

> '*Ae night at e'en a merry core*
> *O' randie, gangrel bodies*
> *In Poosie-Nansie's held the splore,*
> *To drink their orra duddies;*
> *Wi' quaffing and laughing*
> *They ranted an' they sang,*
> *Wi' jumping an' thumping*
> *The vera girdle rang.*'

When at a late hour they rolled home, quite likely they repeated:

> '*We are nae fou, we're nae that fou,*
> *But jist a drappie in our e'e;*
> *The cock may crow the day may dawn,*
> *And ay we'll taste the barley bree.*'

As will be explained in later chapters, the average Scots fisherman of the last century regarded whisky as a sort of sacramental; in fact, there was no bargain which could be struck without the partaking of a wee dram. No business, nor indeed any public or

[26] *History of the Village of Ferryden* (2nd ed. Montrose, 1857), p. 15.
[27] *Social Life of Scotland in the Eighteenth Century* (1909), p. 53.

private event, whether birth, marriage, death or a funeral, could take place without the ritual consumption of whisky. Whisky in generous quantities was supplied to the crews of every herring drifter by the curers who engaged them at the start of the summer season. About 1840 at Auchmithie on the coast of Angus, where the herring season lasted at least six weeks, the six members of a drifter's crew received two whole bottles of whisky every week, but it is related that the fishermen were 'a stout, healthy and generally sober people,' Rather earlier the parish minister of Latheron on the Caithness coast complained bitterly of 'the pernicious effects of the curers giving five to seven gallons of whisky to each boat's crew of four men every night.' He added that in this way 'young men learn drinking habits very early, and in some boats the whole allowance is consumed nightly.'

At Wick, then the chief fishing port in the far north of Scotland, there were forty-five ale-houses in 1840, which the parish minister described as 'Seminaries of Satan and Belial.' Not only in Wick, but in many another port on the East Coast of Scotland during the herring season, the words of the old sailor's chanty could be seen in action:

> '*Whisky makes me pawn my clothes,*
> *Whisky, Johnnie!*
> *Whisky gave me a broken nose,*
> *Whisky for my Johnnie!*
> *Whisky took my brains away,*
> *Whisky, Johnnie!*
> *One more pull, and then belay,*
> *Whisky for my Johnnie!*'

Not only in Scotland, but also in England, France, Belgium, Holland, Germany and the Scandinavian countries, sailors and fishermen were often excused for their inability to keep sober on account of the hardness of their life. Drunkenness among French fishermen was a notorious vice during the eighteenth century. Both the civil and ecclesiastical authorities tried to check it, but with little result. At Saint-Malo during the reign of Louis XV there were at least fifty *débits* around the harbour patronized exclusively by sailors and fishermen, besides more luxurious *hôtelleries* reserved for well-to-do captains and officers. Yet more than one eighteenth century mariner pleaded that drunkenness is not a mortal sin, and that a seafaring life justifies indulgence in alcoholic liquor:

'*Les fatigues de nos travaux très durs, rendent un verre de vin ou d'eau-de-vie necessaires.*'

French fishermen, unlike the majority of English and Scottish ones, consumed as much at sea as on land; for cider, beer, wines and spirits were supplied to the larger vessels by the owners. The annual consumption of alcohol by a Breton or Norman fisherman far exceeded that of the average British fisherman during the last century.

Until well after 1880 the trawler crews of many nations working on the North Sea had been the victims of what were known as 'copers,' sailing vessels fitted out in Dutch, German or Flemish ports as maritime shops. They sold many brands of 'fire-water,' especially gin and brandy, besides clothing and tobacco. It was the National Mission to Deep Sea Fishermen, founded in 1881, that by degrees drove the nails into the coper's coffin by sending out the first of its mission ships; but it was not until 1887 that an international convention at The Hague finally prohibited the sale or barter of spirits on the North Sea, and forced the copers into retirement.

Drunkenness among Scots fishermen became far less common after the first of several 'Revival Movements' in 1859, of which more will be said later. Hymn-singing and prayer meetings superseded drunken orgies in many a town and village along the coast, leading to thrift and a general improvement in the whole way of life.

On the coasts of England and Scotland where inshore fishing from small villages was still carried with lines, drift and trawl nets, or where creels were used for lobsters and crabs, fisher life did not change much. How squalid and uncomfortable it could be, even as late as the first decade of the present century, is revealed by Stephen Reynolds in his two books *Alongshore* and *A Poor Man's House*. He made his home with a typical fisherman's family at Sidmouth, South Devon, and they never ceased to regard their lodger as a 'gentleman,' although later on he became an inshore fisherman himself and shared their life at sea as well as on shore.

Neither the skippers nor the crews of the steam trawlers that gradually succeeded the smacks on the North Sea after 1880, needed special sorts of houses at Hull and Grimsby, for once they stepped ashore they had nothing more to do with their vessels or the fishing gear until they put to sea again. Their wives were not 'fishwives' in the traditional sense, and there was seldom anything in their usually comfortable homes to remind a visitor that the breadwinner was a seafarer, except perhaps a few pictures of fishing vessels. So old customs, taboos and superstitions were forgotten, or deliberately ignored if they were remembered, for they belonged to a way of life that it was better to forget.

In most of the larger ports on the East Coast of Scotland, where many fishermen grew rich during the last decade of the nineteenth century and until the outbreak of the First World War, the herring industry prospered and some magnificent mansions were erected by drifter skippers and members of the crews.

What is interesting about their houses is that they are the logical evolution of the primitive 'but-and-a-ben' described already. They were designed for fisher folk, and every provision was made for the same jobs being done in them as in the older homes. Although the families who owned them lived in the last word of comfort, yet they still lived as fisher folk and were proud to be so. The first thing one usually noticed when passing such houses was that the Venetian blinds in every window were drawn down to what was regarded as the 'correct' level. More often than not there were ferns and plants in ornate brass or porcelain pots inside the heavily curtained windows on either side of the front door, which was frequently made of varnished mahogany. The interior woodwork was usually varnished pitch-pine. Magnificent carved mantelpieces with shelves and columns, sometimes with a framed mirror above and more carving in the surrounding brackets, were fairly common. The wallpapers were sumptuous with much gold in them. In some of these houses one found a stained-glass window half way up the stairs, with the owner's steam drifter depicted in the centre pane. The banisters were invariably carved. The furniture in the two seldom-used sitting rooms was the best that money could buy half a century ago or more. The kitchen always displayed a big range that ate up coal—a far cry to the original open peat fire of earlier times. The display of pots, pans, crockery, china and glass conveyed the sense of the utmost prosperity. But here is the point: the whole or part of the upper floor was given over to a spacious loft for storing herring nets and gear. Between the seasons the nets were mended here. With but few exceptions this loft was approached by an outside stair to avoid taking nets and gear up the inside stairs, thus making dust and dirt.

Both the men and the women who lived in these stately mansions remained real fisher folk in the way they dressed and behaved. Their rise in the social scale made little difference to their outlook on life. Although they were shy to admit it, many of them still believed in old superstitions. Although the majority were devout Presbyterians, yet somewhere in the background was a fear of the old gods of the sea—even of witches and warlocks, kelpies and their like.

A similar rise in standards of living, together with a gradual disappearance of some old customs, taboos and superstitions, went on simultaneously in continental countries. Brittany, however, became the last stronghold of fisher folk-lore, as will be realized from the frequent references to it in subsequent chapters.

Chapter Two

BIRTH AND CHILDHOOD

THE traditional customs associated with child-birth in fisher families were more or less the same in all countries of Northern Europe; for their object was to safeguard the mother and her offspring from evil influences, particularly those coming from the sea.

On the coasts of Finistère and Morbihan, facing the Bay of Biscay, there was a general belief that a mother would suffer more in childbirth when her husband was at sea. At Le Légué, the port of Saint-Brieuc, where half a century ago there were still *goëlettes* and other sailing craft berthed at the long quays; where at an earlier date vessels for the Newfoundland cod fisheries were fitted out; there was a saying:

> *A mer montante de Noël*
> *Garçon qui nait devient capitaine.*

Both here and all along the *Côtes-du-Nord* there was the belief that it was safer for babies to be born on a rising tide; if the tide was ebbing, then quite likely the boy would be drowned.[1] At Saint-Cast, a fishing village on this same coast, the simple folk were sure that if a baby was born when the tide was coming in, there would not be a storm that day, even if everything pointed to it.[2]

When a birth was expected in a fisherman's house on the East Coast of Scotland during the eighteenth and earlier years of the nineteenth centuries, many precautions were taken to ward off diabolical influences, especially the kelpie, a malicious water-sprite. A fir candle or a basket of bread and cheese was placed within the box-bed in the kitchen to keep away fairies.[3] In some fishing villages the midwife put lighted candles at the four corners of the bed. Elsewhere it was the custom to draw a circle according to the course of the sun. Some expectant mothers hung a pair of their husband's trousers at the foot of the bed, because they were believed to possess magical qualities.

The baby having been born, yet more ritual and ceremonial had

[1] cf. Paul Sébillot, in *Archivio per lo studio delle tradizioni*, Vol. V, p. 515.
[2] Sébillot, *Revue des Traditions populaires*, Vol. I, p. 5.
[3] W. Gregor, op. cit., p. 87.

to be carried out. Very often a live coal was thrown into the
water in which the infant was washed. Fire was regarded as a
certain way of keeping off the powers of evil. At Pennan, a tiny
hamlet below steep cliffs on the borders of the counties of Aberdeen
and Banff, if a cradle was borrowed, a live peat was thrown into
it for a few moments before it was used. For similar reasons a torch
was sometimes whirled three times round the head of the mother
and child. Iron or steel were believed to be potent charms. There
is a story of an eighteenth century midwife at Dunrossness in Shetland who took a large table knife and made crosses over the bed
after childbirth.[4] A brooch, known as a 'witch-pin,' was favoured
in Aberdeenshire for driving away fairies. A new-born girl
was sometimes wrapped in a man's shirt; a boy in a woman's
shirt. This was believed to ensure the joys of married life.
When washing a new-born baby, care had to be taken that
the water did not touch the palms of the hands, otherwise the
luck of this world's goods would be washed away. In some places
it was the custom to turn a baby when first dressed three times
heels over head in the nurse's arms, and then shake it three times
with the head down; each operation with a blessing. This was said
to be a certain way of keeping off malicious fairies.[5]

Bread and cheese were almost universal quasi-sacramentals after
the birth of a child. They were eaten at what was called the
'merry meht.' In some places a bannock made of oatmeal, sugar
and milk was baked specially and served to the guests. It was
often known as the 'crying bannock.' The usual custom among the
fisher folk was for each person who called at the house to be given
'a kneeblick o' cheese and breed' and a drink of whisky or ale.[6]

Bastard bairns were supposed to be much more easily frightened
than those born after marriage. The 'kersening' of babies was performed, not only for salvation but much more to drive away evil
spirits. A mother was never safe from the influence of fairies until
she had been 'kirk't' and until her child had been baptized. There
was always the danger that her offspring might be carried away
and a changeling substituted. The saying went: 'A dog's a brute
beast, and a wean's a christen'd creature.'

The fisher folk as well as the farm servants during the latter part
of the eighteenth century used to enjoy Dougal Graham's chap-
book story, *Jockey and Maggy's Courtship*. It is related how when

[4] *Diary of Rev. John Mill* (Edinburgh, 1889), p. 23.
[5] cf. W. Gregor, *An Echo of the Olden Times from the North of Scotland* (Edinburgh, 1874), pp. 90–1.
[6] Gregor, op. cit., p. 85.

the minister said he could not baptize the bastard bairn, the grand-
mother retorted: 'If ye winna christen the wean, ye canna hinn'er
us to cast a cogfu' o' water on 't, and ca't ony thing we like.' Until
a new-born child sneezed there was a fear that fairies might have
got hold of it. After the first sneeze, somebody would say: 'God
sain the bairn, it's no a warlock!'

A child born with a caul [7]—known as a 'silly hoo'—was regarded as very lucky in seafaring families. German and Icelandic
fishermen carefully preserved this portion of the membrane found
on a baby's head, believing that the soul dwelt in it, and that it
prevented drowning.

The belief in the magic of baptism on the coast of Banffshire
during the eighteenth century was universal. Thomas Pennant,
writing in 1769, said: 'The little spectres, called Tarans, or the
souls of unbaptized infants, were often seen flitting among the woods
and secret places, bewailing in soft voices their hard fate.' [8] But all
this had little or nothing to do with Christianity; it was a survival
of the pagan rites which included the use of water, and the bestowal
of a name as safeguards against witches or demons.

The Catholic fisher families on the coast of France had yet more
superstitions connected with child-birth, often much the same as
those current in Calvinist Scotland. In the villages around Saint-
Malo shells were put into the cradle of a fisherman's son; the idea
being that they would influence him to follow in his father's foot-
steps. Some mothers at Le Légué laid their baby boys on seaweed,
hoping that this would make them good fishermen. There was an
old proverb which ran:

'Pour être bon marin et ne pas craindre misère
Sur la flèche if faut coucher en hiver.' [9]

At Saint-Cast an old fisherman's jacket was often laid over a
baby's cradle as a charm against illness, especially rheumatism.
Sometimes the boys were put to sleep in a fish-basket, not for
comfort, but for superstitious reasons. Necklaces made of shells—
limpets being specially favoured—used to be worn by young children as amulets.

[7] Cauls were often worn by Whitby fishermen as a protection from
drowning. As much as £5 was paid for one. (See R. Thurston Hopkins,
Small Sailing Craft (1931), p. 62.)
[8] *A Tour in Scotland*, p. 69; and Lachclan Shaw's Appendix II to Pennant's Tour (1809).
[9] Sébillot, in *Revue des Traditions populaires*, Vol. I, p. 5.

Breton mothers while nursing their babies used to sing them to
sleep with old sea-songs. Here is one of them:

> *'Maman, les p'tits bateaux*
> *Qui vont sur l'eau*
> *Ont-ils des jambes*
> *—Parbleu, mon gros bétias,*
> *s'i'n' n'avaient pas*
> *l'n march'raint pas.'*

Then they would rock them as if they were swimming and say:
'Nage à sec, ou nage à terre,' moving the baby's legs and arms
like those of a swimmer in water.[10]

The games of young fisher children on the coast of Brittany
often related to rowing boats or sailing. They played with fish
which had been caught, especially crabs, pulling off their claws.
Around Cap Fréhel, about half way between Saint-Malo and
Saint-Brieuc, it was the custom on Christmas Eve to gather certain
species of seaweed on the rocks at low tide. While they were being
collected a prayer was recited, then the fishermen returned home,
walking on their hands and feet. On Christmas Day the seaweed
was boiled and the water given to the children to drink. Then they
were told to spit on the weed, and make the sign of the cross.
Gathered at midnight, the beverage was believed to promote intelli-
gence, and the weed itself to give an urge for hard work. There
was a legend that on the night of his birth, the Infant Jesus had
given plants that grow in the sea such power that all who drink of
an infusion made from them would acquire an aptitude for any
job.[11]

The future fishermen grew up and soon became high-spirited
mischievous boys. Their mothers were afraid that they would come
to harm if they wandered about on the rocks, climbed the cliffs, or
went sailing in boats. So they tried to frighten them by warnings
of terrible monsters waiting to eat up children. There were, for
instance, *le gros Nicole* and *le gros Jean.* The former seized hold of
children and shut them up in a cask where they had nothing to eat
but seaweed and only salt water to drink. The latter had claws like
those of a big lobster. He scratched the faces of fisher-boys whom
he met playing on the beach.[12] The mothers at Saint-Cast used to
warn their children of terrible punishments in store if they were

[10] Sébillot, op. cit., Vol. I, pp. 5–6.
[11] cf. Sébillot, in *Archivio,* Vol. V, p. 519.
[12] Sébillot, in *Revue des Traditions populaires,* Vol. I, p. 7.

disobedient. One was to be taken out to the farthest end of the *Ile,* where the fairies would beat them with the long ribbon-like tails of seaweed.[13]

The children in Breton fishing villages grew up with their minds filled with a mixture of superstitions of pagan and Christian origin. One story told by their parents was that God created the sea with a bucket of water and three grains of salt. Around Saint-Malo the older fisher folk used to relate that after the deluge the earth became so dry and parched up that *le bon Dieu* told the birds to fly to Paradise and return each of them with a drop of water in his beak. Such was the origin of the oceans. At Binic, farther west along the coast, there was a legend that many thousands of years ago the sun became jealous of the earth and tried to burn it up. The pious folk prayed hard to God to help them. God bade the saints to tell the sun to go back where he belonged, but he paid no attention to them. Then one of the saints (his name is not mentioned) had the brilliant inspiration that *le bon Dieu* had provided them with natural organs which would annoy the sun. So they took aim and fired urine at the sun for more than eight days, with such violence that he had to retreat. Since then he has kept a safe distance from the earth, and this is one explanation of the origin of the sea, and why it is salt.

There was a tradition at Saint-Malo that waves were the result of a sorcerer jumping into the water from time to time in order to find his magic mill. Another favourite story was that long, long ago the sea was always calm, and sailors had to row everywhere. A certain captain heard that there was a far off country where the winds lived, and he decided to row there and take them captive. It took the crew a long time to reach the country of the winds, but the men managed to pack the winds into sacks, stowed them in the boat, and started on the homeward voyage. One of the sailors was bold enough to peep into a sack. Out rushed the wind, and unfortunately it was a bad one; the fierce *suroît* that blows from the south-west. A gale sprang up. The boat was swamped and the captain and crew drowned. All the other winds, both good and bad, escaped from their sacks, with the result that ever since they have been wandering over the oceans as a constant danger to seafarers.[14]

Listening to such stories as these, children in fisher families around the coast of Brittany and Normandy acquired a wide knowledge of superstitions, and tended to mix them up with legends of

[13] Sébillot, in *Archivio,* Vol. V, p. 518.
[14] This and the previous legend are given by W. Branch Johnson in *Folk Tales of Brittany.*

the saints which were sometimes based more on imagination than
the facts of history. Fathers would tell their sons that tides are
caused by the breathing of a great monster that comes up to the
surface of the water at regular intervals to breathe. At Concarneau
it was said that the tide would always go back to allow the Blessed
Sacrament to be carried around the old town, or *ville close*, built
on an island. At Ploumanac'h, near Perros-Guirec, the fisher folk
were convinced that the tide would always recede to enable pilgrims to visit the shrine of St. Kirek, a sixth century monk, on
the day of his Pardon. Pilgrims to Mont-Saint-Michel were sure
that the archangel would never allow them to be drowned by the
incoming tides. Deep down in his heart, many an old Breton
fisherman believed that although God made the land, it was the
Devil who made the sea. Bretons have always loved the sea, but
at the same time they have feared it. They try to forget it but cannot do so. Hence a ceaseless conflict of feeling and imagination
against the stern necessities of life. The sea is like a woman who
woos her lover, and he is unable to resist her fascination.

So the sons of fishermen grow up, never able to forget the sea,
no matter whether they are indoors or out. They play with toy-
boats in summer, and in winter amuse themselves by pretending
that an upturned table is a ship, and that they are rowing, sailing
or steering. It is related that during the last century the fisher children used to roll naked in the sand before they ran into the sea
to bathe. The sand was supposed to be good for health and made
them strong. Before entering the water they made the sign of the
cross, because they were sure that this would send them straight
to heaven if they were drowned.[15]

As they played together the children would notice any marks on
each other's bodies which their elders had told them were endowed
with some special meanings. On the North East Coast of Scotland
a strong growth of hair on the chest, arms, legs and hands of a
youth prophesied that he would grow into both a strong and con-
tented man. There was the saying:

> *'A hairy man's a happy man,*
> *A hairy wife's a witch.'*

It was easy to find out if anybody was proud. All one had to do
was to take a hair of the head and pull it tightly between the nails
of the first finger and thumb. If it curled, the owner was proud.
A boy with long slender fingers could rest assured that he would

[15] Sébillot, in *Revue des Traditions populaires*, Vol. I, p. 9.

never make a good fisherman; he had better look out for a job in an office ashore. Large hands, on the contrary, indicated bodily strength. If a boy had his second and third toes of nearly equal length, it was certain that he would treat his future wife badly.

The fisher bairns were told that most feelings in their bodies indicated something that would happen sooner or later. For instance, a tingling in the ears was called the 'dead bell.' A buzzing in the ears hinted that somebody was spreading malicious gossip. An itching in the eyes was a warning of tears and sorrow. If one's nose itched, a letter would be received. When there was an itching in the palm of the right hand, it indicated that a friend would soon be shaking hands with you.

Nothing was more welcome than an itching in the left hand, because this proved that money would soon be received. A tickling sensation on the soles of the feet was the warning of a journey about to be made. It was most important to note the days on which one sneezed, for each day counted, either for good or bad:

> *'Sneeze on Monday; sneeze for a letter.*
> *Sneeze on Tuesday; something better.*
> *Sneeze on Wednesday; kiss a stranger.*
> *Sneeze on Thursday; sneeze for danger.*
> *Sneeze on Friday; sneeze for sorrow.*
> *Sneeze on Saturday; kiss your sweetheart to-morrow.'* [16]

Dreams could not be disregarded because they foretold many things; so many, in fact, that it must have been hard to remember them all. A dream about fish meant the arrival of bairns into somebody's family. A nightmare about fire was the warning of very bad news. To dream of a dead person indicated bad weather coming. Oddly enough for an unmarried lad or lass to dream that they were dead was a sign of approaching marriage. These are only a few of the omens given by dreams.

Fisher folk in olden times had an almost universal belief in both good and bad fairies, who had to be propitiated in one way or another. Children were told that the fairies often fished in little boats of their own. They could be seen dressed in green, with little red caps. Their favourite time for fishing was a fine summer morning or evening.[17]

[16] All the above superstitions are recorded by W. Henderson, in *Notes on the Folk-Lore of the Northern Counties of England and the Borders* (1879), pp. 112–13, and 137; also by W. Gregor, op. cit., Chapter VI, 'About the Human Body,' pp. 25–7.
[17] cf. *Folk-Lore Record*, Vol. I, pp. 26–9, and 229–31; also Henderson, op. cit., p. 277.

Here is a story about fairies given by Mr. Gregor:

'One day a fisherwoman with her baby was left a-bed alone, when in came a little man dressed in green. He proceeded at once to lay hold of the baby. The woman knew at once who the little man was and what he intended to do. She uttered the prayer, "God be atween you an me." Out rushed the fairy in a moment, and the woman and her baby were left without further molestation.' [18]

Another and more terrifying story which is given by the same writer, reads as follows:

'A fisherwoman had a fine thriving baby. One day what looked like a beggar woman entered the house. She went to the cradle in which the baby was lying, and handled it under pretence of admiring it. From that day the child did nothing but fret and cry and waste away. This had gone on for some months, when one day a beggar man entered asking alms. As he was getting his alms his eye lighted upon the infant in the cradle. After looking at it for some time he said, "That's nae a bairn; that's an' image; the bairn's been stoun." He immediately set to work to bring back the child. He heaped up a large fire on the hearth, and ordered a black hen to be brought to him. When the fire was blazing at its full strength, he took the hen and held her over the fire. The bird struggled for a little, then escaped from the man's grasp, and flew out by the "lum." The child was restored, and throve every day afterwards.' [19]

Not only on the North East Coast of Scotland was there an almost universal belief in fairies among the fisher folk; stories like the above were told on many parts of the coasts of Brittany, where there existed an equally strong belief in fairies, ghosts, witches and warlocks, of which more will be related.

When a new fishing line was made, with the help of neighbours, the job had to be done without stopping and on a rising tide. When the line was finished everybody was given a nip of whisky, and it was often the custom to 'baptize' the line with a few drops. If a woman came in while the work was in progress, she had to give a silver coin as a contribution towards the drink.[20]

[18] op. cit., p. 61.
[19] ibid., p. 61.
[20] W. Gregor, in *Folk-Lore Journal,* Vol. IV, p. 12; Vol. VI, p. 307.

Club-footed persons were regarded as most unlucky. There is a story that a fisherman at Crovie, a hamlet below the cliffs of Gamrie Bay on the Banffshire coast, was making a new herring net when an 'ill-fitted' man walked into the room. Very little fish was taken the first time it was used, so the owner decided to consult a local sorcerer, who advised that the net should be wound round a pole three times. This charm failed, and the 'wise-man,' having been invoked a second time, said that the line must be destroyed by fire, which was done.[21] Altogether it was a wise precaution to lock the door of a house when a new line or net was being made to prevent any unlucky man or woman casting a spell.

This was done in some fisher communities, e.g. at St. Combs, a village nestling among low sand-hills on the north-easterly tip of Aberdeenshire. Should any unlucky person enter the house when a door was left open, the end of the line was thrown into the fire, or a lighted peat waved round it. At Collieston, south of Peterhead, there was the superstition that the spell cast could be averted by putting the new line into another 'scull' or shallow wicker basket. It appears to have been a fairly general custom if anybody entered the house while a new line was being made to invite the man or woman to put on a few hooks. Having done this, the incomer wished good luck to the job. When baiting a line, nobody would have dared to mention a cat, rat, hare, salmon, or certain other animals which were regarded as unlucky.[22]

The fisher folk who lived in the red granite cottages on the red granite cliffs at Boddam, three miles south of Peterhead, when baiting a line for the first time after a marriage, performed a complicated ritual which involved among other details dragging the line over the floor.[23]

It was looked upon as very risky to count nets or to walk over them, above all if done by somebody with certain physical marks. There is the story of a club-footed fisherman at Pitulie, who met a Broadsea fisherman. The latter was sure that his herring nets had been counted. The only way to avert the spell cast was to draw blood, either from the breast or near the eyes. So the Broadsea fisherman hit the Pitulie man on his forehead, and blood flowed.[24]

To appreciate the atmosphere and background of the typical fisher family in the earlier years of the last century, it is essential to have read some of the chap-books. They were the favourite

[21] W. Gregor, in *Revue des Traditions populaires*, Vol. IV, p. 659.
[22] W. Gregor, *Folk-Lore Journal*, Vol. III, pp. 181, 308; Vol. IV, pp. 12, 13.
[23] W. Gregor, in *Revue des Traditions populaires*, Vol. IV, p. 663.
[24] ibid., p. 663.

D

literature of the working classes, and which were sold by 'travelling merchants.' [25]

> 'They are full of coarse, dramatic vigour, of gross humour in a dialogue of vulgarest Scots. . . . Yet they are valuable from their portraiture with rare fidelity of the tone, speech, talk, habits, morals and immorals of the people. . . . In them is painted with cynical truth how peasants spoke, how they drank, how they courted, how they wedded, and how they forgot to wed; their rude mirth, their gross pleasures; how little they respected the menaces of the Kirk-Session, how disrespectfully they spoke of "Mess John" the minister behind his back; how lightly they regarded uncleanness in thought, speech and behaviour.' [26]

As soon as a boy could read, he revelled in these chap-books, also in the bawdy ballads which his older companions loved to sing. The result was that the average boy brought up in a fisher community on the East Coast of Scotland, as in the country, was familiar with every sort of bawdiness, lewdness and irreverence in his early teens. He was fully aware that after he came of age at sixteen he could look forward to life being made much more enjoyable by interludes of drunkenness and fornication. If he needed any more encouragement in this direction, there were some of the poems by Robert Burns to inspire him.

It seems that a similar Rabelaisian attitude towards life was to be found in French fisher communities, judging from stories which have been handed down. Like the Scottish chap-books, they give the most explicit expression to a robust enjoyment of sex.

There is reason to believe that in most fisher communities on the coasts of France boys underwent an initiation rite before they went to sea. Until about the close of the last century this was soon after the age of nine. This was before they made their first Communion, which until St. Pius X laid down in 1910 that 'the age of discretion' is seven years, more or less, was often delayed even to the age of fourteen. Details of an initiation rite at Audierne, a

---

[25] The earliest chap-books which circulated in Scotland were written by Dougal Graham, the 'skellat bellman' of Glasgow, and appeared after 1754.

[26] Henry Grey Graham, *The Social Life of Scotland in the Eighteenth Century* (1909), p. 188. Writing in 1865, James C. Bertram stated in his *The Harvest of the Sea* that thirty years ago the chap-books were still being sold. He described Dougal Graham's *The History of Buckhaven in Fifeshire, containing the Witty and Entertaining Exploits of Wise Willie and Witty Eppie, the Ale-wife* as 'a collection of very vulgar witticisms tinged with such a dash of obscenity as prevents their being quoted here' (2nd ed. 1869, p. 439).

busy sardine port in Finistère, have been recorded.[27] It is probable that a slight variant of the ritual and ceremonial existed in other fishing ports.

An Audierne fisherman would say to his son one evening: *'Demain tu iras boëtter; je t'ai mis au rôle. . . . Puis, tu seras baptisé.'* The initation rite was known as the *'Baptême du Mousse.'* It was a proud moment for any boy, even if he feared the brutal and coarse treatment described to him by older brothers and companions who had already been 'baptized.' The following morning, carrying a pick-axe and an old wooden *sabot*, he made his way down to the edge of the estuary of the river Goyen at low tide. Here a group of older fisher lads welcomed him effusively; and offered him their tobacco and cigarette papers. Bottles of wine and brandy were opened, and before very long the boy was far from sober. His companions then chanted a parody of an old Breton *cantique* describing the joys of paradise, but in the pleasures of a drunken man (*pligadur an den meo*). The song ended, an introit as it were, the *mousses* proceeded with the actual baptism. They stripped the boy naked if he was too timid or incapable by this time of undressing himself. Some of the lads gathered up handfuls of gravel with which they rubbed the body of their victim. Others scratched his genital organs with bits of glass; so brutally that he often fainted or passed out in a drunken stupor. Next followed the bestowal of a new name, by which he would be known for the rest of his life. Very often the names were associated with the father of the newly baptized; otherwise they stressed some characteristic of the boy himself. His body having been washed and dressed again, the initiated *mousse* was escorted home with the singing of songs describing the rite which had been performed. The father asked what name had been given his son, and pronounced that he was now *'sacré marin.'* The mother knew that from now onwards the boy would depend less and less on her care. It seems that there were instances when the victims never recovered from their initiation rites, but died from their effects. The *'baptème du mousse,'* according to old fishermen in Brittany, was a very ancient ceremony, stories of which had been told them by their fathers and grandfathers. In some places the rite was more simple and consisted of burying the boy in sand up to his waist.

Similar initiation rites were common on the East Coast of Scotland during the last century. Until a lad had been 'brothered' he was not allowed to go to sea or regarded as a full-fledged fisherman. Details of what seems to be a typical 'brothering' rite

[27] H. Le Carguet, in *Revue des Traditions populaires*, Vol. XIV, p. 613.

have been recorded by the Revd. D. McIver, Church of Scotland minister at Eyemouth, Berwickshire, and who published reminiscences of this port in 1906. He relates how some of the older fishermen told him that when they were young, the members of a crew, with whom a boy was to sail, met in a public house. In 1835 Eyemouth boasted fourteen ale-houses for its roughly 1,000 inhabitants. The boy was placed with his back against the wall of the room. Immediately above him, hanging from a block and tackle, attached to a joist in the ceiling, hung a rope with a noose. The rope was put around the boy's neck. Close by was a salted roll and a jug of beer. The boy was told to eat the roll. If he hesitated, one of the men tightened the noose by pulling the rope. While trying to swallow the salty roll, beer was thrown over his face by the skipper. His legs were sprinkled with beer by one of the crew. During this parody of baptism the words 'weather' and 'lee' were repeated. The sprinkling of beer on the face was supposed to symbolize the spray of a 'weather' wave on the bow of a boat; the sprinkling of the legs, the water sweeping over the deck of a fishing boat. While the 'baptism' was in progress the skipper repeated verses meant to inculcate fishing morality, of which the following is a specimen:

> *'From St. Abb's Head tae Flamborough Head,*
> *Whane'er ye cut, be sure ye bend,*
> *Ne'er lea a man wi' a loose end.'* [28]

It is impossible not to suspect that either the old fishermen or the Revd. D. McIver expurgated bits of this narrative in the same way that certain editors of Burns' poems bowdlerized some of his bawdier allusions lest they brought a blush to the cheeks of Victorian readers. It is probable that the Eyemouth initiation rite was even more frank in its allusions to the pleasures of drunkenness and sexual intercourse than the Audierne one. If this was not the case, then fisher folk on the Berwickshire coast early in the last century must have been more prudish than others.

The boys often had to be caught by force before they would submit to be 'brothered.' But once the initiation had been performed they were treated as grown men by their shipmates, as was the case in France. They were given some very odd 'tee-names,' such as 'Old Bar,' 'White Wine,' 'Bobby's Candy,' 'Fly' and 'Tarry.' The use of 'tee-names' have survived in almost all fishing ports on the East Coast of Scotland.[29]

[28] *An Old-Time Fishing Town: Eyemouth* (1906), p. 189.
[29] At Ferryden, Angus, about 1830, the 'tee-names' included the follow-

The old-time Scottish 'brothering' ceremonies usually ended with the crew celebrating the happy event with the consumption of an almost unlimited amount of beer and whisky. Since the initiated youth was now accepted as a real fisherman and treated as such, it was up to him to prove that he had acquired a taste for whisky. From now onwards he could drop into an ale-house or tavern (otherwise a 'howff') and order as many pints of beer or nips of whisky as he could afford. If he had to be helped home 'bleezin-fou' nobody would have been greatly surprised. It was the same in French fishing ports, but with the difference that the *'baptême du mousse'* took place at an earlier age than the 'brothering' in Scotland. There was certainly no Calvinist origin in the Scottish ritual and ceremonial. They were more or less a parody of Catholic baptismal ceremonies, and harked back to pre-Reformation times.[30]

Such then are some of the old fisher customs, taboos and superstitions associated with birth and childhood, and as will be stressed again and again in this book, they resembled each other in most maritime countries of Northern Europe.

ing: Taktime, Red Robbie, Shet Perlie, Tam Tuke, Willie Buckie, Jamie Wee, Water Willie, Lazy Jamie, and Nickie.

More recent ones at Buckie, Banffshire, are: Bosen, Cockie, Shakes, Costie, Curly, Dumpy, Doddam, Peddy, Bodger, Con, Kander, Fosky, Bullan, Dosie, Codlin, Bo, Fling, Stripie, Miss, Coup, and Doddie-Diddie.

[30] At Buckie, and probably elsewhere on the North East Coast of Scotland, should a shipwright apprentice cut himself for the first time with his adze, his mates would say jokingly, 'You are brothered noo.'

Chapter Three

MARRIAGES

BOY and girl marriages were common among fisher folk in most countries until well after the middle of the last century for practical reasons. A fisherman could not be independent until he had a wife and children to help him with his job. He needed sons to go to sea with him if he owned his own boat. If he worked with lines he required healthy, hardworking daughters to help their mother to gather bait, prepare the lines, and to sell fish. Scots law allowed a boy to take a wife after his sixteenth birthday, and in many fisher communities, he had started to raise a family by the time he was seventeen or eighteen.

On the East Coast of Scotland, when superstitions were firmly believed in, there were various ways in which a lad or a lass could find out who was to be the wife or husband. For instance, two peas could be placed upon a burning peat; the one to represent the lad and the other the lass. If the two rested on the peat and burned together with bright flames, whoever had put them there knew for certain that his flame of love would burn with equal brightness. On the other hand, if the two peas jumped away from each other, the lad or lass could be sure that there would be no marriage.

The fisher lassies at Le Pollet, Dieppe, used to look on the beach for a certain white stone which they believed would find them a good husband. The *jeunes filles* around Perros-Guirec on the north coast of Brittany stuck pins into the wooden statue of the sixth century hermit, St. Kirek, which was enshrined in the chapel on the edge of the sea at Ploumanac'h. In the villages between Plougasnou and Trégastel, near Morlaix, a girl used to drop a hair in the holy-water stoup in the oratory at Saint-Jean-du-Doigt, if she wanted to find a husband before the end of a year.[1]

Mr. Gregor recalled that in olden times the fisher lassies at Fraserburgh made use of the following method of divination on Halloween (October 31st).

'They went to the village of Broadsea, which was hard by, and drew a straw from the thatch of one of the houses, the older the thatch so much the better. This straw was taken to

---

[1] *Revue des Traditions populaires*, Vol. XIV, p. 349.

a woman in Fraserburgh who was famed for her wisdom. She broke it; and, if things were to move in the right way with the maiden in her love and marriage, she drew from the broken straw a hair of the same colour as the husband's-to-be.' [2]

It could happen that boys or girls realized that physically they were not ready for marriage; if so, there were several traditional methods for stimulating their sexual powers. One of them, so Mr. Gregor tells us, 'was of such a nature as that it must be passed over in silence.' The following less obscene aphrodisiac, however, appears to have been popular.

'The roots of the orchis were dug up. The old root is exhausted, and when cast into water floats—this is hatred. The new root is heavy, and sinks when thrown into water—this is love, because nothing sinks deeper than love. The root—love—was dried, ground and secretly administered as a potion; strong love was the result.

'Two lozenges were taken, covered with perspiration and stuck together, and given in this form to the one whose love was sought. The eating of them excited strong affection.' [3]

If a fisher lad was shy of the lassies, his companions would tell him to eat plenty of skate, because there was nothing like it for developing his sexual instincts.[4]

Until recent times it was very rare for a fisherman in any country to marry a girl not brought up in a fisher community; again for practical reasons. The only sort of wife useful to him was one who had a good working knowledge of the jobs she would have to do once they set up a home together. There used to be very little contact between fisher folk and country folk. Even in large ports the fisher community kept apart from the other professional classes, and generally lived in a sort of fisher ghetto.

It was this realistic attitude towards mating that recognized premarital sexual intercourse in many a fishing village on the East Coast of Scotland. The first thing a serious minded lad had to ensure was that the lass he fancied could produce bairns, otherwise she would be no use to him as a wife. He could not go far wrong if he followed the advice given by the poet Burns to his younger brother—'to try for intimacy as soon as you feel the first symptoms of the passion. This is the best preservation for one's

[2] *The Folk-Lore of the North-East of Scotland,* p. 86.
[3] ibid., p. 86.
[4] See p. 24.

peace.' Burns had put this advice into the poem entitled 'Nature's Law,' of which the second verse runs:

> *'Great Nature spoke, with air benign:—*
> *"Go on, ye human race;*
> *This lower world I you resign;*
> *Be fruitful and increase.*
> *The liquid fire of strong desire,*
> *I've poured it in each bosom;*
> *Here on this hand does Mankind stand,*
> *And there, is Beauty's blossom." '*

After his sixteenth birthday any fisher lad who was conscious of 'the liquid fire of strong desire' knew that Scots Law allowed him to take a wife, and the sooner he did so the better.

The Presbyterian ministers might denounce the young sinners, and tell them that they would be roasted in great fires and suffer indescribable torments for all eternity, but it made little difference. Burns was a safer guide to faith and morals than Calvin. Sometimes the lads and lassies had to put up with doing public penance for what the kirk regarded as fornication. But only the 'unco-guid' appear to have been scandalized at pre-marital sexual intercourse, which was carried on according to traditional rules, with nothing promiscuous about it.

The Scots fisher lad and lass were fully aware of the form of irregular marriage by co-habitation and repute, which is still legal. If they lived together constantly as husband and wife, and if they were held to be such by the general repute of the neighbourhood, then there was the presumption from which marriage could be inferred. But not many of them in olden times seem to have availed themselves of the rules concerning irregular marriages. It was more usual to have a proper traditional fisher wedding with a minister to tie the knot.

If fisher lads noticed that one of their mates was 'going steady' with a lass, they used to shout at him:

> *'Cockie doss,*
> *Lad and lass*
> *Mairrit in a coal-hole.'*

Another version of the rhyme ran:

> *'Lad and lass*
> *Wi' the fite cockade,*
> *Mairrit in the coal-hole*
> *An' kirkit i' the barn.'*

There were superstitions about colours connected with courting expressed as follows:

> *'Blue*
> *'S love true,*
> *Green*
> *'S love deen*
> *Yellow*
> *'S forsaken.'*

If a lump of burning peat fell from the hearth towards a fisher lad or lass who was wanting to get married, it was a sure sign that all would go well, for there was a saying: 'Fire bodes marriage.' If a would-be bride's garter or apron-string unloosed itself, then she knew that her lover was thinking of her. She never dared to mend the clothes on her back, for that would involve being forsaken by the young man.[5]

The attitude of the average fisher lad towards courtship was probably that of young Sawney, the coalman, who decided to marry Kate, the fish-wife's daughter, which is related in one of Dougal Graham's chap-books. Both mothers wanted the pair to mate, but Sawney had not yet proposed to Kate, who as he said, was 'a sturdy gimmer [young woman] well worth the snoaking [smelling] after.' What's more, she could bring a dowry of 'baith blankets and sheets, a covering and twa cods [pillows], a caff bed and bowster.' He put on his best clothes, with 'his hair cam'd and greased wi' butter, and his face as clean as the cat had licked it.' When Kate told him, 'ye must give a body time to think on 't,' he replied indignantly: 'And do you think I have naething a-do, but come here every other day hoiting [fumbling] after you? It'll no do, I maun be either aff wi' you or on wi' you, either tell me or tak me, for I ken of other twa, and some o' you I will hae . . . I think ye're a cumstrarie [fickle] piece of stuff.'

It may be taken for granted that most fisher lads on the East Coast of Scotland had read and re-read Dougal Graham's *Jockey and Maggy's Courtship,* which always remained the most popular of his chap-books, because of its bawdy details of everything relating to marriage. On his wedding night, Jockey got drunk, as did most of the guests, with the result that he eventually fathered a child by Maggy, his wife, and a bastard by Janet, a servant-girl. So poor Jockey and Janet had to appear before the kirk session for fornication. Jockey's mother told him not to worry and said:

[5] cf. Gregor, op. cit., pp. 86–7.

'My man Johnny, ye'r no the first that has done it, and ye'll no be the last: een mony o' the ministers has done it themselves, hout ey, your father and I did it mony a time.' She took a more charitable view than the kirk session, and remarked that when a couple "hae gotten a bystart, let her and him feed it between them . . . That's better mense [recompense] for a fault than a' your mortifying o' your members, and a' your repenting stools.'

Jockey's mother had the shrewd wit of many a fish wife and was well able to hold her own with the parish minister who insisted that her son must pay a fine and do penance in the kirk. She went so far as to tell the minister that she had been three or four times through a Bible, and could not find any references to a repenting stool; adding: 'Then whar cou'd the first o' them come frae, the Apostles had nane of them.' We are told that the theological discussion was ended by Jockey himself, who 'went an pisht' on the gable of the manse, 'and there was nae mair about it that day.'

It appears that a marriage was usually arranged between the lad and lass without the knowledge of the parents. In some places mothers were first let into the secret before fathers were told. Then it was the business of a father to call on the parents of the lass whom his son proposed to marry, to state what he was worth as to his worldly gear, and to stress his good qualities. If the offer was accepted, an evening was fixed when the couple should meet with their friends, so that the final arrangements could be made. This was known as the 'beukin nicht,' or the 'nicht o' the greeance.' It usually took place on a Friday.

The parents stated what they were prepared to give the future bride and bridegroom. They chose the best-man and the best-maid, also a 'warst' (worst) man and a 'warst' maid. There was much that had to be done; the parish minister had to be informed, for he had to proclaim the 'cries' in the kirk. Then various other details had to be fixed, each with its own date, e.g. 'buskin the joose,' 'buying the dress,' 'measuring and butting the ticking,' and lastly the 'feet-washing.'

The daughter of a well-to-do fisherman was expected to have ready before her marriage a chest-of-drawers, otherwise a 'kist'; also a feather bed, four pairs of white blankets, two coloured ones, two bolsters, four pillows, sheets, one dozen towels, a table-cloth, also crockery and kitchen utensils. Among these was a wooden dish or pail for holding bait when removed from the shells. This was known as a 'sheelin' coug.' A steel blade for taking out mussels also had to be provided. It was the bridegroom's business to supply chairs, a table, and all fishing gear.

As soon as a lass began to think of getting married, she started to collect feathers for her pillows and mattresses. Quite likely some of the lads helped her if they owned guns and shot wildfowl. Once she began to earn money and could save up, she bought a 'kist' (chest), and went on adding to its contents, so that nothing would be lacking to her 'providan' (bridal outfit).

The carrying of the bride's 'kist,' as well as her 'plinisan,' i.e. all her share of the furnishings of the new home, had to be done according to traditional ritual and ceremonial. At least two carts were required. On one cart were placed in order: first the chest-of-drawers, then the mattress over it, next the blankets, and finally the bolsters and pillows. Fisher folk slept between blankets, and did not use linen or cotton sheets. On the other cart were arranged the tubs and domestic utensils. In the wake of the two carts came a procession of women, each one carrying something which it was safer not to put on the carts for fear of it being broken, e.g. a mirror, a picture, or ornaments. It was regarded as most unlucky for the 'plinisan' procession to take place on a Friday, so Thursday was the usual day, since most fisher weddings were held on a Saturday. The bride-to-be locked her 'kist,' and handed the key to the best-man. He placed it in the pocket nearest his heart, if he wore the popular sleeved-waistcoat, otherwise in one of his trouser pockets.

When the cart carrying the 'kist' arrived at the door of the lassie's future home, it was set down upon the doorstep. The best-man took the key from his pocket, unlocked the 'kist,' and lifted the lid full-open three times. At one time it was the custom to utter an incantation at each lifting of the lid. The 'kist' was then carried across the threshold, locked again, and the key handed to the future bride.

In a case where there had been pre-marital intercourse, and it was certain that the lassie had already been 'bairned,' it was better not to inform the minister of this fact when asking him to proclaim the banns. The Saturday night previous to the Sunday on which the first 'cries' were proclaimed in the kirk was the occasion for a feast, to which a few special friends were invited. After this the bride-to-be never dared to appear at the kirk; to have done so would have brought bad luck.

The state of the weather on the marriage day could foretell whether the future would be happy or otherwise. A sunny day was hoped for, though a shower of rain was not regarded as a bad omen. In some fishing villages on the North East Coast of Scotland, after the 'plinisan' had been taken to the house, the box-bed was made up. It was the correct thing for this to be done by one of the bride's sisters, if not, then by some other unmarried woman. Very often a sixpence was nailed to the back of the bed for luck. It was advisable for a woman 'having milk in her breasts' to be asked to arrange the mattress, blankets, bolster and pillows, so that they would be 'magnetized' for the benefit of the future husband and wife.

The usual method of inviting guests to the wedding was for the bride and bridegroom to call at their houses. If the door was closed and nobody there to open it, a cross was made with a bit of chalk. This indicated an invitation. During the three weeks between the first and last proclamations of banns, friends of the bride and bridegroom used to 'rub shoulders' with them whenever they met. This physical contact meant that they wanted to share in the pleasures of the pair after the wedding.

On the evening before the marriage a feet-washing ceremony took place. Some of the bridegroom's friends came to his house, where a large tub was made ready in the kitchen, half filled with water. He was stripped of his stockings and boots; his trousers tucked up well above the knees. His legs were then plunged into the water. One lad took a 'besom' [broom] and with it rubbed them vigorously; another covered them with soot or grease; and a third indulged in coarse gestures and bawdy remarks. After this cere-monial feet-washing there followed much drinking of whisky, to the accompaniment of traditional songs and ballads relating to the pleasures of the sexual act, specimens of which had found their way into the collection of verses known as *The Merry Muses of Caledonia,* first published in 1800, some of them unexpurgated poems by Burns. In a perverted sort of way the traditional Scottish lustration perpetuated the Maundy Thursday washing of feet carried on in Catholic countries during which a hymn is sung, with the refrain: 'Let us love one another from the depths of our hearts. . . . Let there be an end to bitterness and quarrels, an end to strife.'

On the morning of the marriage day, the bride, wearing her wedding dress, repeated the round of houses with her 'best-maid.' The bridegroom, wearing his 'waddin-sark' [shirt]—the gift of the bride—did the same, accompanied by his 'best-man.' As in many fisher communities the parish kirk was some distance from the village, it was more convenient for the wedding to be held in either a school-room or a hall, if not in an alehouse.

It was fairly common for the procession to go round the village after the wedding. As the bride entered her new home, two female friends met her at the door. The one held a towel or napkin, the other a dish filled with bread or scones. The towel was put over the bride's head, and the bread scattered over her. Children ran into the house, picked up the bread and ate it. It was customary for the bride to be led to the hearth, where tongs were handed to her so that she could make up the peat fire. Then the iron crook was swung three times around her head, with a prayer that she would make a good wife.

There are still a few aged fishermen left on the East Coast of Scotland who can recall the marriage feasts that took place during the second half of the nineteenth century, which kept up the traditions of an earlier era. They remember that the meal served was on a generous scale, often consisting of four courses—milk-broth, barley-broth of fowls, beef and mutton, followed by rich puddings served with cream. Beer was the usual drink, and after the banquet the health of the bride and bridegroom was drunk in whisky-punch. Bowl after bowl was made. Each toast was drunk with 'a' the honours three.' Then came dancing. The music was generally provided by a melodeon or sometimes a fiddle. The player gave his services free, but he was allowed to take up a collection in his 'bonnet' and was kept lively with many a dram of whisky. At intervals, bread and cheese, beer and more punch were served. The festivities were kept up until midnight, even until shortly before dawn. The kirk frowned on these matrimonial orgies, but they were too popular to be suppressed.

Dougal Graham relates in *Jockey and Maggy's Courtship* that Jockey's mother provided for his wedding feast, a ewe, three hens and a cock, five pecks of malt ale laced with a pint of treacle 'to make it thicker and a sweeter and maumier [mellow].' She also took care to lay in five pints of whisky 'wherein was garlic and spice, for raisin' o' the wind, and the clearin' o' the water.' On the way back from Jockey's wedding the merry party stopped at every alehouse, where besides drink, haggis was served—richly mixed with bear-meal, spice, mint and onions.

At long last came the traditional ceremonial connected with the 'beddan.' The bride and bridegroom were led back to their house by the now mostly drunken revellers. The bride was undressed and got into bed first. Then a bottle of whiskey and bread and cheese were handed to her. She distributed more food and drink to each person in the kitchen—not that they can have been either hungry or thirsty by this time! After this the bridegroom pulled off one of his stockings and threw it over his left shoulder among the crowd which filled the room. The first who caught it should be the next to be married—if he or she was still single. Finally the bridegroom hauled off his jersey, slipped out of his cloth 'breeks' and woollen drawers, and wearing only his 'waddin sark' got into bed beside his wife. Then the door or curtains of the box-bed were closed, and the happy pair left alone. It was believed that the first to fall asleep would be the first to die. A husband had to take care not to get out of bed before his wife on the morning after their marriage, otherwise he would have to carry the pains and sorrows of child-birth.

In some Scottish fishing villages the day after the marriage, the wives and daughters of the crew to which the husband belonged arrived at the house, each with a basin filled with oatmeal. They brought other presents, such as dried fish, or anything useful for domestic purposes. The donors expected to be entertained by the bride. Some of the ladies seem to have preferred whisky to tea.

Sooner or later the 'kirkin,' otherwise the first attendance of the newly married couple at church, had to be carried out. After this there was another feast, either at the house of the newly married pair or in a tavern. These 'kirkin' orgies on the Lord's Day caused scandal in many places. At Cullen, Banffshire, the following entry was made in the kirk-sessions records of 1785:

'It was observed by some members of session that a practice prevailed in the parish of people's meeting together in the publick-houses upon the Lord's Day for what they called kirking feasts, where they sat and drank and gave offence to their Christian neighbours.' [6]

What were known as 'penny weddings' or 'penny bridals'—very popular among the poorer classes during the eighteenth and early nineteenth centuries—were another cause of scandal to 'gweed livin' fowk.' It was the custom for each guest to make an offering in money for the food and drink supplied. In some villages, where there was no large room or public hall, a 'penny bridal' was spread over several houses. In 1708 the Kirk-session at Cullen 'nolified' that:

'considering that many abuses are committed at penny weddings by a confluence of idle people that gather themselves mainly to hear the musick did and do hereby enact that whoever afterwards shall have pypers att their wedding shall forfeit their pauns [pledges] and that they should not meet in a change hoss [tavern] the Sunday after their marriage under the same pain.' [7]

[6] Gregor, op. cit., p. 97.
[7] ibid., p. 93.

These week-end matrimonial 'bottle-parties' invariably ended with what was called 'promiscuous dancing between men and women.' The first dance was the 'shaimit-reel,' performed by the bride, her maidens, and bridegroom and his best young men. Sometimes the bride fixed a marriage favour on the right arm of her partner, and so did the best maid. Or there might be a repetition of the 'shaimit-reel' with other lads and lassies, followed by the gift of more favours. Dancing and drinking usually continued throughout Saturday evening until the early hours of Sunday morning. Whisky-punch flowed freely. Old and young men and women got 'bleezin' fou.' The fiddler, stimulated by whisky, went on playing furiously. A typical fisher penny-wedding in the early years of the last century is pictured for us in the following verse:

'But ben the hoose the ample floor is cleared,
To make the merry place both long and wide;
And in a corner, chairs and stools are reared,
Where pulpit-high the fiddler sits in pride,
With jolly mug of porter by his side,
Snuff in his hose, and mettle in his hands,
Making the busy fiddlestick to ride
A nimble jig along the roset bands;
At which the dancers jump as moved by magic wands.
And from ilk youthful and most living pair
Comes forth at stolen times the slander glance—
While smiles and becks begin as the warm reels advance.
And every lass, with handkerchief on lap,
Doth spread the dainties which the bride hath stored:
Such as ane Penny Wedding may afford—
Spendings and cheese, and bannocks scoundered brown,
And butter taken from the kit's good hoard,
And tea well masked in a pot of great renown,
Mixed with ane drop of gin, the nervous draught to crown.' [8]

The Presbyterian ministers had been denouncing Penny Weddings from not long after the Reformed Religion was established in Scotland. In 1631 the Presbytery of Strathbogie (Huntly, Aberdeenshire) issued the following warning, and so did many other Presbyteries during the next two hundred years, but without much result:

'In respect of the many abuses and disorders that fall out

---

[8] James Bowick, quoted by D. H. Edwards, *Amongst the Fisher Folks of Usan and Ferryden* (Brechin, 1921), p. 225.

at penny bridals, especially of plays and drunkenness, it is
ordained that no person hereafter shall be married who shall not
promise that there will be no abuse at their bridal, under pain of
ten pounds.' [9]

At Newhaven, near Edinburgh, fisher marriages always took
place on a Friday, usually regarded as an unlucky day, but this
gave everybody a better chance to enjoy themselves than if a
wedding took place on a Saturday. To have held it earlier in the
week would have meant being away from sea. Here is a first-hand
record of a typical Newhaven marriage about the middle of the
last century.

'The guests are invited two or three days beforehand by the
happy couple, *in propriis personis,* and means are taken to remind
their friends again of the ceremony on the joyous day. At the
proper time the parties meet—the lad in his best blue suit, and the
lass and all the other maidens dressed in white—and walk to the
manse or church, as the case may be, or the minister is "trysted" to
come to the bride's father's residence. There is a great dinner provided for the happy occasion, usually served at a small inn or
public-house when there is a very large party. All the delicacies
which can be thought of are procured: fish, flesh and fowl; porter,
ale and whisky are all to be had at these banquets, not forgetting
the universal dish of skate, which is produced at all fisher marriages.[10] After dinner comes the collection, when the best-man, or
someone of the company, goes round and gets a shilling or a sixpence from each. This is the mode of celebrating a penny wedding,
and all are welcome who like to attend, the bidding being general.
The evening winds up, so far as the young folks are concerned,
with unlimited dancing. In fact dancing at one time used to be
the favourite recreation of the fisher-folk. In a dull season they
would dance for "luck," in a plentiful season for joy—anything
served as an excuse for a dance. On the wedding night the old
folks sit and enjoy themselves with a bowl of punch and a smoke,
talking of old times and old fishing adventures, storms, miraculous
hauls, etc.; in short, like old military and naval veterans they have
a strong *penchant* "to fight their battles o'er again." The fun grows
fast and furious with all concerned, till the tired body gives warning that it is time to desist, and by and by all retire, and life in the
fishing village resumes its old jog-trot.' [11]

[9] *Extracts from the Presbytery Book of Strathbogie,* p. 4 (Spalding Club,
Aberdeen, 1843).
[10] As stated already, skate was believed to arouse the sexual instincts.
[11] James G. Bertram, *The Harvest of the Sea* (2nd ed. 1869), pp. 421–2.

At Collieston, a now moribund fishing village about half-way between Aberdeen and Peterhead, after the usual marriage feast everybody adjourned to the Links at the end of Forvie Sands, where they danced the intricate 'Lang Reel o' Collieston' to the strains of a fiddle. It was a 'long reel' in every sense, and continued while pair after pair dropped off, until none were left dancing but the bride and bridegroom. Writing in *The Banffshire Journal* about a hundred years ago, a spectator recorded that:

'to see the lang reel o' Collieston danced on the greensward under the blue canopy of heaven on a sweet afternoon in summer, is a treat worth going many miles to enjoy. Not only would the eye enjoy a rare feast, but what with the sweet music of the violin, the merry song of the lark in mid-heaven right overhead, the ringing guffaws of the juvenile spectators, the clapping of hands, and the loud *hoochs* and whoops of the dancing fishermen, all co-mingling and co-mingled with the murmur of the billows breaking among the rocks, the ear would have a banquet of no ordinary kind nor of every-day occurrence.'

The parish minister about the same time had a high opinion of his fishermen, who, so he recorded, were 'superior to other working tradesmen, never interfered in the politics of the day, and who are most regular attendants at the ordinances of religion.' [12]

The fisher weddings at Buckie, Banffshire, about the middle of the last century tended to be rowdy, and what else could have been expected when most of the bridegrooms were lads of seventeen or eighteen? Previous to a fisher marriage the kirk session exacted a pledge of half a guinea that no rioting or fighting would take place. If, as the result of too much whisky having been consumed, there was brawling or even bloodshed, the pledge was given to the poor, but if the party managed to behave itself, the money was returned to the bridegroom the following Sunday.

At Avoch, Ross-shire, fisher weddings usually took place on a Friday and never before midday. Here, as in some other places, Friday was selected because it allowed the whole of Saturday and Sunday for keeping up the festivities before going to sea again on Monday morning. In towns and villages where herring fishing was carried on, marriages generally took place at the end of the autumn season, when there was more money to spend.

In Catholic countries on the continent of Europe, fisher weddings used to be more religious in character than those on the East

[12] *New Statistical Account of Scotland,* Vol. XII, p. 589.

E

Coast of Scotland. Very often there was a nuptial Mass. On the Ile-de-Sein, for instance, the prospective bride and bridegroom each used to give a banquet to their near relatives, where the guests contributed to their share of the food and drink. The following morning the bridal pair went to Holy Communion at Mass, and in the evening there was another festive meal, followed by a dance. Next morning Mass was celebrated in the parish church for departed relations, after which the bride and bridegroom visited the cemetery to pray for the repose of the souls of their next of kin. For a whole month the newly-wedded wife abstained from work in the fields.

It was always the custom at Boulogne-sur-Mer (as it still is in most Scottish fisher communities) for the bridegroom's boat to be adorned with flags and bunting. His new home, and even other houses in the same street, used to be adorned with flowers and flags. Many a festive fisher wedding with a nuptial Mass has taken place in the church of St. Pierre-des-Marins, looking down on the harbour; even more in the parish church at Le Portel, a village on the cliffs near Boulogne, where most of the inhabitants are fisher folk and still pious Catholics.

At Boulogne, just as in ports in Banffshire and elsewhere on the East Coast of Scotland, the wives always took charge of the money earned by their husbands or unmarried sons. If a Boulogne fish-wife was in a good mood she conducted her man to a *patisserie,* and treated him to sweets or pastries. On the other hand, if she wanted to make her neighbours aware that there had been a difference of opinion, she arranged her elegant coiffure (known as a *'beau soleil'*) in a particular manner.[13]

There were recognized limits to bridal bondage and petticoat government. In some of the less sophisticated fisher communities in Normandy and Brittany, if it became known that a man had allowed himself to be beaten by his wife, other fishermen tied a basket on his back, and dragged him from tavern to tavern. His punishment continued until he had stood what were regarded as enough rounds of drinks. Another custom was to take a cart on which was hung a pair of trousers at the end of a pole. The woman who had beaten her husband got on the cart, and the neighbours cried out: *'Par ma fa, mon fu' 'est ielle qui porte les brées!'* The hen-pecked husband was put on another cart, adorned by a petticoat hanging on a pole, indicating that the roles of man and woman had been inverted.

This particular story comes from Saint-Jacut-de-la-Mer, west of

---

[13] cf. Sébillot, op. cit., p. 56.

Saint-Malo, where in the 1880s many curious old customs survived. It is related that one of the leading fishermen had been
caught while having illicit relations with a girl nick-named *'la
Taupe'* (the mole), because she was very dark-skinned. So a cart
was dragged round the village decorated with moles and mackerel.
Lying on straw was a figure dressed to represent the culprit.[14]

Chapter Four

FISHER FESTIVALS, PILGRIMAGES AND BLESSINGS OF THE SEA

THE piety of fisher folk has manifested itself in Catholic countries mainly in the form of processions and visits to favourite shrines. The instinct survived in Protestant countries, and in Scotland found its normal outlet in visits to holy wells; also in keeping up many pagan festivals, some connected with fire-worship.

Even to-day the French fisherman, who may call himself a Communist, often clings to certain superstitions of Catholic origin. It is not surprising to find him with a rosary in his pocket, or worn round his neck as an amulet. Somewhere at the back of his mind is a dim idea of Mary, Mother of God, Star of the Sea—a spiritual lighthouse, a heavenly pilot, a divine protectress, a merciful and kind mother who forgives and understands the weakness of human nature—to be called upon in moments of danger and distress.

It is in Brittany that one finds most traces of traditional maritime piety. In former times few men ventured to embark for the New-foundland cod-fisheries without a pilgrimage to a local shrine of Our Lady. In most village churches a special Mass was celebrated before the *'départ des Terre-Neuvas'* at the altar of Our Lady. Throughout the summer months mothers, grandmothers, wives and sweethearts went on praying for the safe return home of the crews of the *'goëlettes,'* working on the other side of the Atlantic. The flames of innumerable votive candles flickered like spiritual light-houses before the image of the Mother of God in every village church on the coast; more especially in the pilgrimage shrines of Notre-Dame-de-l'Epine (Saint-Brieuc), Notre-Dame-de-la-Landrais (Miniac), Notre-Dame-de-l'Esperance (Mont Dol), Notre-Dame-des-Flots (Rothéneuf), Notre-Dame-du-Bois-Renou (La Gouesnière), Notre-Dame-de-la-Garde (Saint-Benoit des Ondes), to mention but a few around Saint-Malo.

In the autumn when the cod fisheries were over, it was a fairly common sight during the last century to meet whole crews walking bare-footed along the roads, wearing either their fisherman's clothes, or else merely trousers and shirt—an act of gratitude and penitence for preservation from dangers at sea. On the day of the 'Pardon' at Notre-Dame de Bon Voyage at Plogoff, not far from the Pointe-du-Raz in Finistère, the Audierne fishermen and others from adjacent villages used to walk both ways with bare feet. If they had been preserved from shipwreck, they wore the same clothes as when their escape took place. It is recalled that sometimes they jumped into the sea, and walked into the chapel dripping wet. There is the story that certain Breton fishermen early in the last century made a vow during a storm at sea that, if they were saved, they would climb the lofty spire of the fifteenth century church of Notre-Dame-Folgoët (Finistère), and let themselves hang downwards with their arms extended.[1]

At the mouth of the River Odet, opposite Benodet, there is a little chapel dedicated to the Blessed Virgin, not far from the village of Sainte-Marine. In the days of sail, when a crew was wind-bound, it was the custom for two men to go on foot to the chapel and ask Our Lady to change the direction of the wind. Before doing so they swept and cleaned the chapel, collected the dust, and threw it in the direction they wanted the wind to blow.[2]

After the Blessed Virgin, Breton fishermen have always put their trust in St. Anne, the mother of Mary, who according to a very dubious legend was born in Brittany and somehow found her way to Palestine. After the death of St. Joachim, she is alleged to have returned to the land of her birth, and ended her days in a hermitage on the edge of the Bay of Douarnenez, where now stands the Chapelle Sainte-Anne-de-la-Palue. A much frequented 'Pardon' takes place there every year on the last Sunday in August.[3]

Since 1623 the most famous shrine in Brittany dedicated to the mother of Mary has been at Sainte-Anne-d'Auray (Morbihan). Devotion to her among seafarers has generally taken the form of a vow made during a storm at sea, or other occasions of danger, to make a pilgrimage to one of her shrines if they are saved. Very often the *voeu* included going barefoot and bare-headed, dressed only in shirt and trousers, and fasting on bread and water.

Fishermen on the coast of Normandy have their own favourite shrines. Until modern times on certain days in the year they made pilgrimages to Notre-Dame-de-Grâce, Honfleur; Notre-Dame-de-la-

---

[1] Mabasque, *Notions sur les Côtes-du-Nord,* Vol. I, p. 308.
[2] L. F. Sauvé, in *Mélusine,* Vol. II, col. 207.
[3] Some folk-lore historians maintain that St. Anne is merely the Christian substitute for Anès, the pagan goddess of the sea, worshipped by the Bretons before they became Christians. The cult of St. Anne, who was venerated at Constantinople in 550, had spread to Rome by the eighth century. The Franciscans were keeping her feast in 1263, but it did not become obligatory throughout the Latin Church until 1548. There is a French tradition that St. Lazarus brought her relics from Palestine to Provence; also another legend that St. Peter took her body from Jerusalem to Rome!

Délivrance, near Caen; and to many a small chapel dedicated to Our Lady, including those near Le Havre, Dieppe and Fécamp. For more than a thousand years a miraculous statue of Our Lady, alleged to have drifted ashore in a boat without oars or sails, was venerated at Boulogne-sur-Mer. In March and September every year fisher folk have gone on pilgrimage to Notre-Dame-des-Dunes at Dunkirk. In the limited space of this book it would be impossible to give anything like a complete list of the shrines of Our Lady all round the coasts of France, Portugal, Spain and Italy, and other Catholic countries in Europe which have been resorted to by fishermen and other seafarers.

Sometimes the piety recorded is very naïve, for instance, on the North Coast of Spain the fishermen who had made a vow to Our Lady of Perpetual Succour, used to say to her: 'Virgin, if you do not give us a fish we will give you a barrel of vinegar,' i.e., instead of a barrel of wine which they would have normally offered at this particular shrine.[4]

It would take up too much space to mention all the saints venerated by Breton fisher folk. Almost every district and port has its own patron or patroness. St. Clement I (Pope and Martyr), St. Brieuc (Brioc), St. Lunaire (Leonorus), St. Jacut and St. Cast—the last four Celtic monks—are popular along the coast between Saint-Malo and Cap Fréhel. Around Paimpol and Tréguier the honours are shared between St. Yves (Ivo), St. Gildas and St. Gonéry. St. Kirek has no competitors at Perros-Guirec and Ploumanc'h. St. Barbara tries to get a look in around Roscoff, but St. Pol-de-Léon (Paul Aurelian) easily beats her. North-east of Morlaix, St. John the Baptist heads the list, because one of his fingers is said to be enshrined at Saint-Jean-du-Doigt. In Finistère the fisher folk venerate a crowd of holy men and women, with priority to St. Illtyd and St. Pol-de-Léon. Among others are St. Non (mother of St. David of Wales), St. Viaud, St. Tromeur and St. Tronoân. St. Gildass the Wise is popular around the Golfe de Morbihan, because he spent some years as a hermit of the Ile Houat.

The fishermen at Audierne, one of the chief sardine ports in Finistère, have St. Evette (Eva or Thumette) as their particular patroness. According to the local legend she escaped shipwreck on this wild coast, and crossed the Bay in a stone trough. There is a story of a fisherman who made a pilgrimage to Auray and complained to St. Anne that he was too old ever to do it again. She told him not to bother, because at his home port he had

[4] B. Vigon, *Folk-Lore de la Mar*, Vol. VIII.

St. Evette who wielded quite as much power in heaven as she did.[5]

In Catholic countries most fisher communities have their annual festivals, which combine religious devotion with secular revelry. They usually take place on the feast day of the saint to whom the parish church is dedicated, and very often this is the occasion for a blessing of the fishing fleet, with fireworks in the evening. In more than one port on the French Riviera it used to be the custom for the fishermen to process through the streets with an old boat decorated with flags, which they finally burned to the accompaniment of dancing and singing.[6]

A typical simple sort of festival in a small fisher community on the coast of Normandy is that at Etretat in 1880. Before High Mass a group of fishermen carried into the parish church a model ship resting on a pyramid of flowers. They placed it on a large loaf of bread, which was afterwards cut up and distributed as *pain-bénit*. Each man held a tallow candle. Their leader, the local sail-maker, intoned a traditional *cantique,* and prayed that the boats would be preserved from attacks by the Turks and pirates! [7]

Here is a first-hand description of the annual festival off the Ile-de-Groix, on the coast of Morbihan, about 130 years ago, which took place on June 24, the feast of St. John the Baptist.

'The fishing boats of all the adjacent parishes went in procession to take part in this solemn ceremony, and to invoke Notre-Dame-de-l'Armor that the sardines might be abundant and of good quality. Crowded with men, women and children dressed in their Sunday clothes was a vast fleet of every sort of craft. At the head of each "squadron" sailed the boat in which were the clergy, their vestments making a brilliant note of colour in the sunshine, the cross held up aloft and the banner of each parish waving in the breeze. Having arrived near the middle of the strait which separates the Ile-de-Groix from the mainland, the sea was blessed in turn by all the priests who were on board the boats, accompanied by the singing of chants and hymns by the onlookers, together with fervent ejaculations to "Notre Dame" and "Madame Sainte Anne." ' [8]

Functions of the same kind are still carried out in many fishing ports on the coasts of France, Portugal, Spain and Italy. In the

---

[5] cf. P. Sébillot, op. cit., pp. 89–90.
[6] L. Roubaudi, *Nice et ses environs,* in *Mélusine,* Vol. II, p. 342.
[7] F. S. Bassett, *Legends of the Sea* (1885), p. 407, from a letter bv an eye-witness.
[8] L. Kérardven, *Guionvac 'h* (1835), pp. 80–5.

days of sail the annual blessing of the vessels before they crossed
the Atlantic to take part in the cod fisheries on the Newfoundland
Banks used to be a most impressive sight at Saint-Malo and
Fécamp. It was the same at Paimpol before the '*goelëttes*' sailed for
Iceland in February, not returning to their home port until the
first mists of autumn.[9] On that day every vessel was blessed before
it left the harbour. In honour of the occasion a *reposoir*, always
of the same design, in imitation of a grotto with rocks, was erected
on the quays, surrounded by trophies of anchors, oars and nets,
with the image of Notre-Dame-de-Bon-Voyage from the parish
church enthroned on it. The Blessed Sacrament, followed by a
slowly moving procession of mothers, grandmothers, wives and
sweethearts, was carried round the harbour, where lay all the Iceland schooners, decorated with flags. Their crews saluted as the
priest paused for a moment and raised the monstrance to bless
each vessel in turn.

Even thirty years ago the *Pardon des Terre-Neuvas* at Saint-Malo
was still one of the most impressive religious functions connected
with ships to be found anywhere in the world. Fifty or more three-
master barquentines, all gay with flags and bunting, were berthed
in the port. Accompanied by crowds of clergy, the Archbishop of
Rennes embarked on a motor-boat after High Mass in the Cathedral. Slowly moving round the great basin, where the quays were
crowded with sightseers, including friends and relations of the crews,
he blessed each vessel in turn, most of the fishermen having climbed
aloft into the rigging. A similar function took place at Fécamp
before the trawlers left for the cod fisheries, and during the afternoon the fishermen, their wives and families, climbed the steep
path to the chapel of Notre-Dame-de-Salut on the cliffs. Its walls
are covered with crude paintings of vessels and ship-models, placed
there in thanksgiving after preservation from drowning or safe
return from a long voyage. Here they prayed for those who were
about to start on their long voyages across the Atlantic to Newfoundland, Greenland or Iceland.

At Berck, originally a small fisher community six miles south of
Le Touquet, before it developed into a fashionable *plage* about a
hundred years ago, there used to be a blessing of the sea every year
on a Sunday in September; typical of functions in many another
French fishing village, some of which have survived. A boat was
prepared for the priest from which he could bless the sea and
preach a sermon. Four skippers carried a statue of St. Peter the
Fisherman in the procession. Other statues were carried by mem-

[9] This was described by Pierre Loti in his novel, *Pêcheur d'Islande* (1886).

bers of confraternities, and banners floated in the breeze. Three young fisher lassies were dressed to represent Faith, Hope and Charity.

Until the middle of the last century Étretat on the coast of Normandy was a picturesque fishing village, popular with artists. Every year on August 15th, the feast of the Assumption of Our Lady, the *curé* preceded by the *enfants de choeur*, left the church carrying a silver cross. The procession made its way to the shingly beach below the chalk cliffs. Here the priest recited a prayer, with everybody kneeling around him. Then he made the sign of the cross over the water and said: 'In the name of the Father, Son and the Holy Ghost, I bless the sea. I put under the protection of Mary our boats and their crews, their nets, sails and ropes.' After this the fisher folk chanted the Litanies of Our Lady, and the procession returned to the church in silence.[10]

In the fishing ports on the coast of Flanders the feast of SS. Peter and Paul, June 29th, was favoured for the annual blessing of the sea and the boats, carried out with more or less the same ritual and ceremonial. In some parts of Brittany it used to be the custom for the clergy to go in procession on one of the three Rogation Days preceding Ascension Day to the cemetery, where prayers were said for the repose of the souls of seamen and fishermen.

At Audierne and other ports in Finistère, priests were regarded as necessary to break the spell which an evil spirit, known as '*le Bosj*,' cast upon boats and lobster pots if certain traditional pagan methods had failed. Among the latter was to steal some object from another boat. This done, the *Bosj* would leave the vessel and board the other. An alternative method was to steal a handful of oat straw and take it on board the boat without anybody noticing it. At night, when the boat was at sea, one of the men set the straw alight, and cried: 'The Devil is on board.' The rest of the crew, roused from sleep by the smell of smoke, knocked everything about. The *Bosj*, thoroughly alarmed, jumped into the sea.[11]

If it was decided to call in a priest to exorcise the *Bosj*, the boat was given a thorough clean, decorated with flags and banners, and anchored in the harbour. Followed to the quay by a crowd of fisher folk, the priest was rowed out to the vessel. Having performed the ritual blessing, the *patron* offered him a glass of wine, which he was bound to drink. The bottle was then passed round the crew in turn, and if anything remained of the contents, was handed across

[10] cf. Alphonse Karr, *Le chemin le plus court*, p. 61.
[11] H. le Carguet, in *Revue des Traditions populaires*, Vol. IV, p. 537.

to other boats. The priest was rowed back to the shore, the anchor raised, and the vessel put to sea. As a reward for services rendered, the priest was always given the next large lobster caught.[12]

The intensely Catholic fisher folk on the Ile-de-Sein, if they found that the blessing of the sea by the local priests had not brought them the hoped-for good luck when shooting creels for lobsters, reverted to a pagan rite. This involved stealing some nets, burning their corks, breaking a plate, and putting the pieces into the lobster-pots instead of bait. The bark of their wooden rings had to be singed with fire. However great might be their faith in Our Lady and local saints, some women on the coast of Finistère used to make their husbands wear a *louzou* or magic bag, alleged to drive away evil spirits and bring good luck while fishing.[13]

Almost every French fisher community had its own *cantique* addressing Our Lady, sung at annual blessings of the sea and on other occasions, each with a lilting chorus. At Port-en-Bessin the refrain of the *cantique des matelots* runs:

> *Vierge Sainte, aimable Marie,*
> *Doux réconfort des matelots,*
> *Daignez conserver notre vie*
> *Lorsque nous sommes sur les flots.*

At Fécamp every fisherman loved to join in the refrain of the *cantique des Terre-Neuvas:*

> *Astre béni du marin,*
> *Conduis ma barque au rivage:*
> *Garde-moi de tout naufrage,*
> *Blanche étoile du matin.*

The Boulogne crews had their own *cantique* with the chorus:

> *Salut, Patronne séculaire,*
> *De nos flots, de notre cité.*
> *Guide-nous astre tutélaire*
> *Jusqu'au port de l'éternité.*

At Paimpol and in the adjacent villages the fisher folk chanted:

> *Notre-Dame-de-la-Garde,*
> *Patronne des matelots,*
> *Soyez notre sauvegarde,*
> *Contre la fureur des flots*
> *Gardez les matelots.*

---

[12] ibid.
[13] H. le Carguet, op. cit., Vol. IV, p. 467.

The sardine fishermen at Tréboul, opposite Douarnenez had a six verse *cantique* with the refrain:

> *Vogue, barque legère,*
> *Sous l'astre tutelaire,*
> *Notre-Dame-des-Flots,*
> *Notre puissante Mère,*
> *Des pauvres matelots*
> *Entendra la prière.*

These popular hymns, and many more in the same style, sum up as it were the simple piety of French fisher folk, found in almost every coastal village until living memory, and in some places still far from dead.

Traces of pre-Reformation Catholic piety survived in a few fisher communities in England long after the sixteenth century. At Penzance, and in certain other places in Cornwall, the fishermen continued to light fires on June 24th, the feast of St. John the Baptist, and danced around them. At Staithes, north of Whitby in Yorkshire, it was the custom on June 29th, St. Peter's day, for the fishermen to decorate their cobles, and to perform certain traditional rites, after which a festive meal took place.[14] Orcadian fishermen used to sprinkle their boats with water on November 1st, though they had long since ceased to keep it as the feast of All Saints. This rite, known as 'fore-spoking,' also included marking a cross on the boats with tar.[15]

Folkestone was another port where Catholic piety lapsed into pagan superstition after the Reformation. Until fairly recently it was the custom among the fishermen to choose eight of the largest and best whiting from every boat on returning from that fishing, and selling them apart from the rest. The money was set aside for a drunken revel on Christmas Eve, known as the 'Rumbald.' Probably very few of the crews of the then numerous two-masted luggers which made up the fleet a hundred years ago knew that in Catholic times the money thus collected was donated to a chapel between Folkestone and Hythe, dedicated to St. Rumwold, long since demolished.[16] If a fisherman did not take part in this annual orgy, it was believed that he would be drowned during the coming

---

[14] cf. Brand, *Popular Antiquities* (1849), Vol. I, pp. 319, 338.
[15] cf. W. Jones, *Credulities, Past and Present* (1880), p. 107; and F. S. Bassett, *Legends of the Sea* (1885), p. 401.
[16] Rumwold was the son of a seventh century Northumbrian prince, who died shortly after becoming a Christian.

year. Eventually it was given up, but December 24th was still called 'Rumbald Night.'

It is recorded that at Clovelly, on the North Coast of Devon, the fisher folk, who belonged to the Church of England, held a special service every year, at which Psalm 107 was sung or said, because of its references to those 'that go down to the sea in ships, that do business in great waters.' They prayed that God would send them an abundance of fish.[17]

On the East Coast of Scotland the fisher folk during the seventeenth and eighteenth centuries continued to make pilgrimages to certain holy wells, although the Reformed Church had strictly forbidden these and other superstitious practices as early as 1579. One of the most popular was the Lady Well at Orton on Speyside, otherwise known as Our Lady of Grace. St. Fittick's well, near the Bay of Nigg, south of Aberdeen, remained a place of pilgrimage; so was St. Wallak's well, near Cromarty. St. Olaf's well at Cruden Bay, Aberdeenshire, was credited with the power of warding off diseases, and the people recited the verse:

> St. Olave's well, low by the sea,
> Where pest nor plague shall ever be.

Just as in Catholic countries, there were blessings of fishing boats, but in post-Reformation Scotland they were associated for the most part with pagan fire festivals. They have survived in the 'burning of the Clavie' at Burghead on the coast of Moray. On the afternoon of Hogmanay young men prepare a tar barrel by sawing it in two. The smaller part is fixed into a six-foot long salmon fisherman's stake, called the 'spoke.' According to tradition no hammer can be used to drive in the connecting nail, which is fixed by a stone. The barrel is filled with tar and wood, a place being left for a burning peat. Towards sunset the Clavie is set alight. The 'Clavie-bearer' starts to go round the village with his blazing burden. Halts are made and burning faggots thrown into open doors to bring good luck to the householders. The procession ends on the headland outside the village, where the Clavie is set on a stone pillar, known as the 'Doorie,' and fresh fuel piled on it. In olden times it went on burning all night, but now after burning for about half an hour, the blazing mass is broken up. People scramble for the embers which are preserved as amulets.

During the seventeenth and eighteenth centuries there were other places on the Moray Firth Coast where 'clavies,' i.e. torches, were

[17] cf. F. S. Bassett, *Legends of the Sea* (1885), p. 401.

burned on New Year's Eve. Their kirk sessions records contain references to fire torches being 'superstitiously carried about the boats.' In 1689 a young lad at Burghead was cited for having made 'a burning clavie, paying a superstitious worship, and blessing the boats after the old heathenish custom.' Other seamen were accused of the same offence, which included carrying meat and drink to the boats—a propitiatory sacrifice to the sea gods. But the fishermen paid scant attention to the admonitions of their ministers. In 1875, when Burghead had about fifty fishing vessels, and about 200 men forming their crews, the Clavie was still being carried to the harbour, so that the boats could be purified of all malignant influences.

There are stories of torches being burned and offerings made to fishing boats at Findhorn, Lossiemouth, and other ports on the North East Coast of Scotland. On New Year's Eve young men at Stonehaven, Kincardineshire, still wander around the streets waving fireballs until they burn out. The original object—to-day almost forgotten—was to drive away evil spirits from the fishing boats. At Lerwick in Shetland and elsewhere there are variants of the New Year fire ceremonial. All had the same object as the blessings of the sea and boats with holy water in Catholic countries, i.e. to purge air, earth and sea of unclean and hostile influences.

Fire has always been a religious symbol. In certain pagan religions the mysterious nature and irresistible power of this element frequently caused it to be adored as a god. Christianity adopted this belief, but denied the divine title to heat and light, making them symbols of the divinity, which enlightens and warms humanity. This symbolism led naturally to the liturgical rite by which the Church on Easter Eve celebrates the mystery of the Death and Resurrection of Christ, of which the extinguished and rekindled fire furnishes the expressive image. All lights having been extinguished, the new fire is kindled from a flint, and blessed with prayer. After this the lights are lit again. At one time it was the custom almost all over Europe to light bonfires on Easter Eve, yet as early as the eighth century the Church had condemned certain superstitions connected with the kindling of fire by friction, which had survived from pagan times. In Britain this was known as 'Needfire,' and it was produced by the rubbing together of two pieces of wood. After the Reformation the peasantry on the East Coast of Scotland made widespread use of needfire, although the Presbyterian ministers tried to stop it. Both the farmers and fishermen resorted to needfire at certain times of the year; the latter usually at the start of a fishing season.

The ritual and ceremonial resembled those which are observed in the Western and Eastern Churches on Easter Eve. First of all every fire in the neighbourhood had to be extinguished; often those in every house within sight of the spot where the new fire was to be kindled. In a fisher community each boat's crew often did this before the start of a fishing season. The new fire was then cast on the boats, nets and lines. There is a record of this being done at Garmouth at the mouth of the Spey in 1664.[18]

A much later instance of the kindling of needfire among fisher folk comes from Reay, a village on the North Coast of Caithness. Here it was the custom for a boat's crew to meet in the skipper's house after dark. The peat fire on the hearth was extinguished. Each man took his share in rubbing together two pieces of wood, and the friction never ceased until a spark had been produced, and shavings set alight. Then a peat was kindled, and when enough were blazing, each man took one back to his own home to light a new fire.[19]

Once lit, a new fire was not allowed to go out until some special occasion when the rite had to be performed again. In certain fishing villages, it was regarded as most unlucky to take fire from one house to another on New Year's morning. The story is told that a Buckie fisherman met a boy coming out of his house that day with a glowing peat to enable a shoemaker to light the fire in his shop. The fisherman cursed his wife for allowing the lad to take away the fire, assuring her that he would have bad luck for the rest of the year. But in this case the sea gods were fickle, and sent an abundance of fish.[20]

There were other traditional customs connected with New Year's Day. On the Banffshire coast the fisher folk about the middle of the last century went down to the shore, filled a jug with salt water and carried it home with a certain kind of seaweed. They sprinkled the water over the fire, and put the seaweed above the doors and corners of their houses.[21] Having done this they felt sure of good luck for the rest of the year.

On Hogmanay evening most families used to 'rist' their fires by covering up the live peats with ashes. The first thing to do on New Year's morning was to see if there was any mark like a human foot in the ashes, with the toes pointing to the door. This was regarded as an omen of death in the family before the end of the

[18] cf. W. Cramond, *The Church of Speymouth*, p. 30.

[19] cf. Alexander Carmichael, *Carmina Gadelica* (Edinburgh, 1900), Vol. II, pp. 340ff.

[20] cf. W. Cramond, *Reminiscences of the Old Town of Cullen* (Aberdeen, 1882), p. 45.

[21] cf. G. Hutchison, *Days of Yore* (Buckie, 1887), p. 27.

year. Another death warning was if a newly-lit peat rolled away from the hearth that same morning.[22]

On the south side of the Moray Firth the more superstitious fishermen were afraid to go to sea after the New Year until they had shed blood. It is related that fishermen at Portessie, near Buckie, would hit anybody who dared to wish them good luck before going to sea, for by shedding blood the spell cast would be averted. If it was too stormy for the boats to put to sea on New Year's Day, men who owned guns went to the beach before dawn, waiting for the sight of any living creature they could wound or kill, so as to have proof of shedding blood. Otherwise the blood of a fish caught served as a sacrifice to the gods. There was always a rush to get to sea, because of the belief that the first boat that reached the fishing ground, shot lines and hauled them, and gutted fish, would have the best luck during the coming year. The skipper's son was allowed what was known as the 'eel-shot,' i.e. the first fish caught and gutted on New Year's Day.

It seems that it was long ago that the French taught the Scots to transfer to New Year's Day and its eve the feast of Yule, formerly celebrated on Christmas Day. In the North East of Scotland, however, the conservative character of the people made them go on observing Christmas privately after the Reformed Kirk had forbidden the keeping of all Christian festivals.[23]

'First footing' after midnight had its traditional customs. The darker the hair of the visitor, the more welcome he was. No red-haired man or woman was wanted, neither were the deformed, crippled, flat-footed, those with turned-in toes, and definitely not grave-diggers.

The essential part of the ritual of first-footing in olden times consisted of bringing a gift of some kind. It usually took the form of a bottle of whisky, but in some places shortbread, oatcakes, 'sweeties' or 'sowens' were equally acceptable tokens.[24] Sometimes there was a ceremonial sprinkling of the door of a house with sowens; elsewhere the mixture was smeared on the door in revenge for non-admittance. Boys and girls in many a fishing village used to approach each house, singing a song of at least eight four-line verses, one of which ran:

> *Rise up, gweed wife an' shak yer feathers,*
> *Dinna think that we're beggars.*
> *It's hae for wersels that we've to beg*
> *It's an aul' wif wi' a crystal leg.*

[22] cf. W. Gregor, op. cit., p. 160.

[23] It was not until 1871 that January 1 became a Bank Holiday in Scotland.

[24] 'Sowens' is a sort of porridge, made of meal and husks, left to steep till it becomes sour.

An alternative ending in some Banffshire coastal villages was:

> *We're only bairnies come to play*
> *Rise up an' gee'se oor hogmanay.*

Until living memory this song was sung by parties of bairns at Portsoy and the adjacent fisher communities.

Symbolic of the human sacrifices in pagan times was the so-called 'Burry-Man' in some fishing towns and villages on the East Coast of Scotland. In a sense the burry-man was a scape-goat, offered up to the sea gods when the fishing had failed. At Buckie about a hundred years ago the fishermen used to dress up a cooper in a flannel shirt with burrs stuck all over it, and drag him through the streets on a hand barrow. At Fraserburgh in the 1860s the ceremonial was more elaborate. The victim was mounted on horseback. Not only were his clothes covered with burrs, but a number of red herrings were suspended from his hat, head downwards. Preceded by a piper, the burry-man rode round the town, followed by a crowd of fishermen, cheering and singing, hoping that this ancient rite would change the luck of the fishing.[25] In other ports the burry-man went on foot, wearing a high-crowned hat, with herrings hung round it by their tails. He was preceded by two men on horseback, the first fantastically dressed, the second playing the bagpipes. The burry-man procession had the specific object of 'raising the herring.'[26]

At South Queensferry, on the Firth of Forth, the procession was held annually about Lammas, the first week in August, on the day preceding the fair. Here the victim was a lad dressed in loose garments covered over with burrs.[27]

In both Catholic and Protestant countries, fishermen used to make offerings of fish, just as is the custom with pagan fishermen who want to propitiate their gods. For instance, at Buarca on the North West Coast of Spain the fishermen believed that their luck depended on offering part of their catch to Our Lady of the Rosary.[28] The same custom existed at Great Yarmouth and Gorleston long after the Reformation.

The custom of offering sacrifices to sea-gods survived in remote maritime communities. For instance, Martin in his *Description of the Western Islands of Scotland*, first published in 1705, relates that

[25] John Cranna, *Fisher Life in Buchan*, p. 12.
[26] cf. W. Gregor, op. cit., p. 145.
[27] E. B. Simpson, *Folk-Lore in Lowland Scotland* (1908), p. 128f.
[28] cf. *Boletin Folklorico español*, p. 44.

in at least one crofter-fisher community on the Isle of Lewis, sacrifice was offered to a deity called 'Shony' on Halloween. The people gathered after dark at the Kirk of St. Mulvay, with plenty of home-brewed ale. Then a chosen man, playing the part of priest, waded into the sea carrying a cup of ale. He chanted in Gaelic: 'Shony, I offer you this ale, hoping that you will be so kind as to send us plenty of seaweed for enriching our ground the ensuing year.' The ale was poured into the sea as a libation. After the man got back to the shore, everybody entered the kirk. A candle left on the spot where the altar used to stand in Catholic times was suddenly extinguished—symbolic, as it were, that the sacrifice was over. The rest of the night was spent in dancing and drinking.[29]

---

[29] Dr. A. McBain records in his *Celtic Mythology and Religion* (p. 171) that after the Presbyterian ministers had finally managed to suppress this neo-pagan ceremony, some people 'proceeded in spring to the end of a long reef and invoked "Briannuil" to send a strong north wind to drive plenty sea-ware ashore.'
Belief in sea-deities and demons survived in the Hebrides long after they had been forgotten on the East Coast of Scotland.

F

Chapter Five

BLACK AND WHITE MAGIC—WITCHES AND WITCHCRAFT

UNTIL fairly recent times there was a firm belief in both black and white magic, not only among the semi-pagan nominal Presbyterian fisher-folk on the East Coast of Scotland, but also those in Catholic Brittany and Normandy. As Sir James Fraser wrote:

'We should deceive ourselves if we imagined that the belief in witchcraft is even now dead in the mass of the people. On the contrary there is ample evidence to show that it only hibernates under the chilling influence of rationalism, and that it would start into active life if that influence were ever seriously released. The truth seems to be that to this day the peasant remains a pagan and savage at heart: his civilisation is merely a thin veneer which the hard knocks of life soon abrade, exposing the solid core of paganism and savagery below.' [1]

Devil compacts were common enough in Catholic Brittany as well as in Presbyterian Scotland. Sometimes they were made at midnight in a graveyard, when men or women became bound to devote themselves to the service of Satan, either for a limited period, or for the rest of their lives. This gave them the power

'to do almost everything man could conceive—to control the elements, to send disease on man or beast, to make crops infertile, to destroy them by wind or rain, to amass as much wealth as they wished to spend on their evil passions—in short, to do what wicked work they set their minds to. A wild wanton life did such lead, often with the appearance of unbounded wealth and happiness far beyond the reach of most men. Their whole time seemed one round of success and joy.' [2]

There are stories of Breton captains of 'terre-neuvas' who sold their souls to Satan, or who committed mortal sins in order to have luck at fishing. For instance, the captain of the Saint-Marcan,

---

[1] *The Golden Bough*, **Part VII**, *Balder the Beautiful* (1913), Vol. I, pp. viiiff.
[2] Gregor, op. cit., p. 74.

having done very badly for some time, exclaimed one day: 'I would gladly sell my soul if only I could catch a fish.' [3] Soon afterwards his luck changed in an almost miraculous manner, but eventually his ship was lost in a tempest. Another tale, told at Saint-Cast, concerned the skipper of a boat who made a similar devil compact, and caught plenty of fish, after which Satan himself towed the boat back to Saint-Malo in four days. [4]

Then there is the story of how the captain of a certain *'terreneuva,'* finding his vessel becalmed, went down to the cabin and started to curse before the statuette of Our Lady, blaming her for the lack of wind. He hit the image with his fist, and threw it on to the deck, where it lay broken. Soon after this a breeze arose, the vessel was damaged, the captain was drowned, and the crew caught hardly any cod. The men were convinced that their *patron* had sold his soul to the Devil. Some even went so far as to swear that they had seen his ghost skimming over the waves in the form of a burning fire, and that the moment a fish was on the line they felt an invisible hand which let it go free again. [5]

On the intensely Catholic Ile-de-Sein there used to be the conviction that certain women had what was known as *'le don de vouer,'* i.e. the power of communicating with the Devil or his emissaries; in other words that they were witches. Fishermen alleged that they had seen these women on dark nights launching mysterious boats (*bag-sorcèrs*) to enable them to take part in a witches' sabbath or coven, known as a *groach'hed.* If anybody on the island had an enemy and wished to be rid of him he could do so by making a contract with one of these *voyeuses,* though she usually demanded a generous fee. She made three trips in a *bag-sorcèr*, took part in three *groac'hed,* and each time handed over to the demons of the winds and the sea some object belonging to the doomed man. Old fishermen around the coast of Finistère told stories of the mysterious disappearance of individuals, and never doubted that it was due to the machinations of women who had *'le don de vouer.'* [6]

Both the agricultural and seafaring classes in the Channel Islands retained a strong belief in the active agency of Satan until well on in the last century. Victor Hugo's novel *Les Travailleurs de la Mer,*

---

[3] This Breton Catholic skipper was in the tradition of Peter, the Galilean fisherman who 'fell to calling down curses on himself and swearing, "I know nothing of the man,"' after his speech has betrayed him (Matthew 26:69–75; Mark 14:66–72; Luke 12:54–62; John 18:17–27).
[4] *La France Maritime,* Vol. III, p. 276.
[5] *Revue des Traditions populaires,* Vol. XII, p. 392.
[6] cf. W. Branch Johnson, *Folk-Tales of Brittany.*

published in 1866, centres round Gilliatt, who lived in a haunted house, went fishing, and always caught fish. He prowled around at night, conversed with sorcerers and haunted the druidical stones of L'Ancresse or the fairy caverns. This sinister, bachelor fisherman was feared by all his neighbours. Some people swore that they had seen him talking to a toad. There are no toads on Guernsey, so this toad must have swum from Jersey! Hugo states:

'Sorcerers are common in Guernsey. They exercise their profession in profound indifference to the enlightenment of this century. Some of their practices are shocking. They set gold boiling, gather herbs at midnight, and cast the evil eye upon cattle. When the people consult them they send for bottles containing "water of the sick," and mutter mysteriously, "the water has a sad look." In 1857, one of them discovered, in water of this kind, seven demons. They are feared by all. . . . Some sorcerers are obliging, and for two or three guineas will take on themselves the complaint from which you suffer. . . . Others cure diseases by merely tying a handkerchief around the patient's loins, a remedy so simple that it is astonishing that no one had yet thought of it.' [7]

The last sorcerer to be burned alive on Guernsey was in 1747, but Victor Hugo relates that in his time they were condemned to eight weeks' imprisonment if discovered working their spells—four weeks on bread and water, the remainder of the time in solitary confinement.

The modern traveller, moving up the East Coast of Scotland, either by rail or road, passes many places which in olden times were alleged to be associated with devil-worship, witches and warlocks. About 1590 a certain Alice Sampson confessed that the Devil attended a meeting of witches in the now ruined parish kirk at North Berwick, where he said that King James VI was his greatest enemy in the world. She also admitted

'sailing with certain of her complices out of North Berwick in a boat like a chimney (the Devil passing before them like a rick of hay) to a ship called *The Grace of God*, in the which she entered, and the Devil caused her drink wine, and gave her other cheer; and at her being there she saw not the mariners, neither saw they her; and when they came away the Devil raised an evil wind, he being under the ship, and caused the ship to perish.' [8]

[7] op. cit., Book I, Chapter 2.
[8] Quoted by P. W. Sergeant, *Witches and Warlocks* (1936), p. 261.

Barbara Napier confessed to having taken part in a gathering of seven score of witches in North Berwick kirk on All Hallows' Eve, where there was dancing in the kirkyard. On June 25, 1591, Euphemia McCalyan was burned alive, with other witches, having been convicted of attending covens at North Berwick and elsewhere, and trying to raise storms to wreck the royal ship, etc.[9]

During the eighteenth century the fisher folk at Buckhaven, Fife, believed firmly in black and white magic.[10] On the coasts of Angus and the Mearns there were many strange superstitions in the fisher communities, especially at Stonehaven. Here no skipper would put to sea without asking an 'ancient dame' to propitiate the spirits of the winds. During the seventeenth century there was a famous witch at Cove, a fishing village a few miles north of Stonehaven, who claimed to cure fevers. Aberdeen seems to have been regarded as a hot-bed of black and white magic, judging from the frequent references in the kirk sessions records from the close of the sixteenth century. Witches and sorcerers used to dance around the Fish Cross at Halloween, and people said that Satan himself directed the orgies. Strange rites were performed when a new boat was launched. Fire festivals were very popular.

The Peterhead fisher folk had their 'spae-wives' who cast spells, usually with knotted cords. Still alive in this port in 1819 was a middle-aged man said to be well acquainted with the occult sciences. Fraserburgh, another large fishing port on the North East Coast of Aberdeenshire, had its own witches, some of whom were believed to be in league with Satanic powers.

The south side of the Moray Firth seems to have been the chief coastal district for devil compacts and witchcraft. Moving west, Rosehearty, Pennan, Macduff, Banff, Whitehills, Portsoy, Cullen, and Buckie are full of memories of black and white magic. On the Bin Hill above Buckie witches' covens used to be held. The fisher folk in all the small villages of Banffshire and on the coast of Moray were as superstitious as the country folk. Burghead especially was always a stronghold of strange rites, above all fire festivals. The small county of Nairn during the seventeenth century had many notorious witches. The parish kirk at Nairn, close to the 'fisher toun,' was the scene of more than one convention of witches at midnight like those on the Ile-de-Sein.[11]

[9] According to a rough estimate, 3,400 persons in Scotland were condemned to death for witchcraft during the sixteenth and seventeenth centuries. The last execution of a witch was in 1727, when a woman was burnt on the charge of having ridden her own daughter to the covens, the said daughter having been transformed into a pony and shod by the devil (cf. Chambers, *Domestic Annals of Scotland*, iii, 541).

[10] See p. 105.   [11] See p. 83.

On the north side of the Moray Firth we find similar superstitions in almost every fisher community right up to the Pentland
Firth. Satan was a very real person at Cromarty, Portmahomack,
Dunbeath and Scrabster—to mention but a few places. Black and
white magic played a part in most families, so some of the parish
records suggest. This was even more the case in the islands of
Orkney and Shetland, where superstitions handed down from
remote Scandinavian ancestors retained their hold over the people.

Many alleged witches lived in the Orkneys during the seventeenth and eighteenth centuries. Jane Forsyth, known as the Storm
Witch of Westray, began consorting with Satan at the age of twenty,
foretelling disasters at sea, and curing diseases. After an adven-
turous career she went to Liverpool and never returned to her
native islands. Janet Rendel of Rigga, known as the Spitting Witch;
Kitty Grieve and Mary Richart of Rendall; Annie Taylor (the Cat
Witch) of Sanday; all practised black and white magic during the
seventeenth century.[12]

Mr. Gregor tells us that:

'The witch was usually an old woman who lived in a lonely
house by herself, and kept all her affairs very much to herself.
Her power was derived from Satan, was very great, and ranged
over almost everything. By various ways she could cause disease
in man and beast; raise storms to destroy crops, sink ships, and
do other destructive work; steal cows' milk, and keep herself
well supplied with milk and butter though she had no cows. To
do this last she was able to turn herself into a hare. At times,
however, she used her power for the benefit of those who pleased
her. She could cure diseases, discover stolen goods, and tell who
the thief was. Such a woman was dreaded, and all her neighbours
tried to live on good terms with her, bore from her what they
would bear from no one else, and, if she asked a favour, would
have granted it, however much it cost to do so. If one was
unfortunate enough to fall out with her, something untoward was
sure to happen to the offender, and that too in no long time after
the quarrel. . . . Sometimes the witch, instead of sending upon
her enemy a single disaster, set herself to give all manner of
petty annoyances, dogging him in all directions.' [13]

It was said that the power of witchcraft was handed down from

---

[12] cf. W. R. Mackintosh, *Around the Orkney Peat-Fires* (3rd ed. Kirkwall, 1914), pp. 293–345.
[13] op. cit., p. 71.

one generation to another in certain families, and more rarely was possessed by men.[14]

The names of some of the women who possessed *'le don de vouer'* have been preserved, also those of a few men who practised the 'black airt' as it was called. Among the latter was John Philp of Banff who had a great reputation as a wizard. Margaret Davidson, also resident at Banff, got into trouble in 1615 for performing indecent fertility rites. Janet Wishart bewitched as well as healed folk on the coast of Kincardinshire. Andro Mann was a much sought after healer on the Banffshire coast. Dorothy Calder, who was a witch living at Forres, on one occasion encircled some salmon fishermen with a knotted straw rope. Agnes Duff seems to have found plenty of fisher folk at Fraserburgh ready to believe in the charms she cast by melted lead and water. As late as 1819 there were said to be a man and woman at Peterhead who could cure diseases, reveal secrets, and even make the dead rise from their graves.

About the middle of the last century, both at Macduff and at Rosehearty, two fisher communities on the south side of the Moray Firth, there were 'wise women' who threw stones into the sea as a protective charm, white stones being regarded as the luckiest. They perpetuated the tradition set by Margaret Spence at Banff, who in 1674 was convicted of casting water seven times out of the sea towards the royal burgh, and five stones into the sea at the time of Sunday worship. She protested 'on her soul's salvation' that she did this to prevent an epidemic of fever spreading.[15] Isobel Gowdie and William Kerrow, both of Elgin, used verbal charms against fevers early in the seventeenth century, which were probably resorted to by the superstitious fisher folk at Stotfield (as Lossiemouth was then called), which at that date was the port of Elgin.[16] Here we find a mixture of pagan and Christian charms, for one of the verses recited by these magicians ran:

> *'The quaking fever and the trembling fever*
> *And the sea fever and the land fever,*
> *Both and the head fever and the heart fever,*

[14] cf. Henderson, op. cit., pp. 180ff., and *Folk-Lore Record*, Vol. I, pp. 23–6.

[15] cf. W. Cramond, *The Annals of Banff* (New Spalding Club), Vol. II, p. 50.

[16] In 1670 the Stotfield fishermen were cited before the Kirk Session of Kineddar for the 'idolatrous custom of carrying lighted torches round their boats on New Year's Eve'; also 'warned against going to the superstitious place called the Chapel of Grace' (see p. 76).

And all the fevers that God created,
In St. John's name, St. Peter's name,
And all the saints of heaven's name,
Our Lord Jesus Christ's name.' [17]

The Catholic fisher folk on the Côtes-du-Nord in Brittany had much the same sort of superstitions connected with cures for sickness and diseases as the nominal Presbyterian ones on the Moray Firth Coast in Scotland. For instance, there was a fairly widespread belief that a weed found on the shells of a certain species of crabs could cure epilepsy, but only if it were collected at three o'clock in the morning of Easter Day by a man with a clear conscience. At Erquy, a village west of Cap Fréhel, it was said that the weed found on a gurnet's head cured certain diseases. The fairies were supposed to cultivate various kinds of seaweed, which were gathered on the rocks, boiled down, and made into magic ointments.[18]

There was a regular succession of male and female healers who practised their arts among the superstitious fisher families along the East Coast of Scotland from early in the seventeenth century. Their charms took various forms. Some consisted in the repetition of certain words, usually in verse, which were recited over the patient. Other magic formulas were texts from the Bible, written on a piece of paper and carried about by the sick person, often in a bag suspended from the neck. Threads of various colours, usually with knots on them, were sold as charms. Magic feathers found a ready market. Black wool was supposed to have a special curative value. Some witches cured diseases with charmed water; others with earth taken from graves. Silver, iron, lead and other metals were also used, and miracles might take place if they were properly 'magnetized.' Stones were popular and regarded as amulets when carried around the neck. Sometimes the witches prescribed magic circles, which took various forms, e.g. a circular wreath of woodbine, or of knotted straw rope. Passing through a circle of stones was another way to regain health.[19] But it seems that as a general rule ointments or potions made from alleged magic herbs were most popular.

The more intransigent Scottish Reformers, with their often

---

[17] (Spelling modernized.) Cramond, op. cit., Vol. II, p. 182.
[18] cf. Sébillot, in *Archivio per lo studio dell tradizioni popolari*, pp. 518, 576.
[19] cf. J. M. McPherson, *Primitive Beliefs in the North-East of Scotland*, pp. 235–62.

exaggerated belief in the power of the Devil, had raised him to almost the same omnipotence as God. The inevitable result was that many people in the seventeenth and eighteenth centuries accepted the metaphysical system known as dualism; holding that good and evil are the outcome or product of separate and equally ultimate first causes. Since the *Westminster Confession,* ratified by the General Assembly of the Church of Scotland in 1647, had made it an article of faith that God had willed the positive reprobation of the damned to whom salvation is denied from all eternity, without any fault of their own; and that Christ died only for the elect, because since Adam's fall God has not wanted the salvation of all men; the logical conclusion was that as nobody could be *sure* if he or she was of the elect, it was safer to keep the right side of Satan. So it was that 'Auld Sandy,' 'Auld Cloutie,' or 'The Auld Goodman' became a sort of familiar spirit, treated with respect, and even with affection.

Until the middle of the last century most parishes along the East Coast of Scotland still had a plot of land dedicated to the Devil and left uncultivated.[20] The fisher folk at Eyemouth, Burnmouth and St. Abbs were familiar with the verse repeated in Berwickshire:

> *'The Moss is soft on clootie's craft,*
> *And bonny's the sod o' the Goodman's taft*
> *And if ye bide there till the sun is set,*
> *The Goodman will catch you in his net.'* [21]

At King Edward, about four miles inland from Macduff, on the Banffshire coast, the so-called 'Given Ground' was never touched with spade or plough until early in the nineteenth century. All these innumerable shrines of Satan had been dedicated by traditional ritual and ceremonial. Sometimes the local laird donated the land in perpetuity. Stones were thrown on the 'Goodman's Croft,' symbolizing that man had renounced his right to the land.[22]

Judging from their Records, there were few parishes in the North East of Scotland which did not have a Goodman's fold or croft during the seventeenth and eighteenth centuries. The kirk sessions tried but usually failed to suppress the sorcery alleged to take place from time to time at one or other 'Halie man's rig.' The fisher and farming families who resorted to them really did

---

[20] Known under various names, e.g. the Halyman's Rig, the Goodman's Fauld, the Gi'en Rig, the Deevil's Croft, the Black Faulie (sheep-fold).
[21] Henderson, op. cit., p. 278.
[22] cf. McPherson, op. cit., pp. 134–41.

believe that the offerings made there propitiated a mysterious Higher Power, probably Satan.

The hell-fire clubs which existed in the same districts were rather different in character. The meetings are said to have taken the form of orgies of blasphemy and drunkenness. Stories were told that the members celebrated an obscene Communion service once a year, always about midnight. At Turriff, for instance, only about ten miles south of the nearest point on the Banffshire coast, the Presbytery in 1647 got a certain Andrew Hogs to confess that 'on the Lord's Day he had drunken the Devil's good health at the Cross of Turriff, confusion to the parson at Turriff, and to the Covenant, and with him John Burnet, Gilbert Harper and Donald McKeddie, piper, piping to the drink, and William Kay who came all from the house of Dalgaty.' [23]

Within eight miles of the coast of Kincardineshire during the seventeenth century it was reported that the Devil had often been seen for the greater part of a winter prowling around on the Garrol Hill near Durris. Now few fisher folk were more superstitious than those at Stonehaven, and it was their usual custom to pay a 'wise woman' before they went to sea, to bring them the requisite breeze of wind.[24] So it may be presumed that they took good care to keep on friendly terms with Satan. Even if they never had the privilege of meeting him in person, they must have been told what he looked like by others. One Aberdeenshire man described 'ow he wiz a gey decent like chiel, if he hidna had a terrible heid o' horns an fearfu' lang hairy legs wi' great cloven feet, but Lord, man, he hid a terrible smell o' brimstane.' [25]

[23] James Brebner, *In Turriff Presbytery 200 years ago* (n.d.).
[24] James M. Mackinlay, *Folk-Lore of Scottish Lochs and Springs* (Glasgow, 1893), p. 221.
[25] Gregor, *Folk-Lore Journal*, Vol. VII, p. 289.

Chapter Six

FISHING VESSELS

SO long as fishing vessels depended on sails and oars it was only to be expected that countless superstitions would exist, because their movements were at the mercy of nature. Nature could be kind but it was often cruel. Both the sea and wind gods had to be propitiated. The French luggers, bisquines, chasse-marées, goëlettes, terre-neuvas, crabbers, sardine-boats, etc., had to be safeguarded before they put to sea, with blessings by priests. Scots fishermen took equal care that their skiffs, skaffies, baldies, and even the later 'fifies' and 'zulus,' were not built and launched without carrying out certain traditional semi-pagan rites and ceremonies. It was the same in every maritime country in Europe, no matter whether the religion was Catholic or Protestant.

The fishermen at Boulogne-sur-Mer used to be certain that they would have bad luck if a new lugger, trawler or drifter was a long time being built, or if alterations were made in the design after the keel was laid down. It was not wise to have this done on a Friday. The day having been fixed, the *patron* and his crew met at the boatbuilding yard, where a shipwright knocked the first nail (tied with a red ribbon) into the keel. After this all adjourned to a café for the first of many rounds of drinks which would continue until the new boat was launched.[1]

On the north coast of Brittany it was the custom to give the keel of a new boat a mystical 'sprinkling' by the owner standing a round of drinks after it had been laid down. In Scotland there was a superstition that the look of the first shavings from a saw could predict the good or bad luck in store for a new boat.[2] The timbers used had to be chosen carefully, because there were both 'male' and 'female' species. It was believed that a boat built of 'female' wood sailed faster during the night than during the day.[3] Some Scottish skippers believed that to ensure good luck for new

[1] P. Sébillot, in *Revue des Traditions populaires*, Vol. XIV, p. 103.

[2] In some yards when a new boat was laid down, the owner used to hint to the builder to place a gold sovereign in a recess in the keel (within the stem onset joint). The builder kept this secret, and never revealed where he had hidden the coin.

[3] W. Gregor, in *Folk-Lore Journal*, Vol. IV, p. 10. 'She-oak,' or chestnut, is lighter than white-oak. Fishermen believed that 'she-oak' had 'powers.'

boats it was necessary for the owner's wife to dab on the first spot of tar.[4]

In the fishing ports along the Côtes-du-Nord of Brittany, once the bows of a new boat were finished, she was given her first 'baptism' with sea-water. The following verse was recited:

> *Bateau, n'aie pas peur de cette eau,*
> *Plonge dedans comme un oiseau,*
> *Et te relève aussitôt;*
> *Mais crains et fuis les rochers,*
> *Car si tu vas les trouver,*
> *Sois sùr d'être brisé.*[5]

Then on the day the boat was launched the crew chanted:

> *Bateau, que pour la première fois nous*
> *lancons à l'eau,*
> *Porte chance à tes matelots.*

Once she was afloat a flag was hung over each bulwark, and the men recited the verse:

> *Pour que le bateau porte bien la voile,*
> *Nous suspendons ces morceaux de toile*
> *A chacun de ses côtés*
> *Pour qu'l ne peut (sic) chavirer.*
> *Je demande que ce bateau*
> *Vogue sur l'eau et sur la mer,*
> *Comme les oiseaux volent dans l'air.*[6]

In Lower Brittany one hour before high tide was the correct time for launching a new fishing boat; in Higher Brittany, low water was chosen. She had always to be launched bows first, the belief being that if launched stern first she would not be able to turn easily. At Yport in Normandy, once a new fishing boat was launched on the shingly beach below the chalk cliffs, her bow was turned round so that she could salute a statue of Our Lady.[7]

In Catholic countries it was the conviction that a vessel not blessed by a priest was bound to be unlucky. Very often it was

[4] ibid.
[5] P. Sébillot, *Le Folk-Lore des Pêcheurs*, p. 137.
[6] ibid., pp. 138–9.
[7] cf. *La France Maritime*, Vol. I, p. 246.

difficult to find a crew for a new fishing boat which had not been 'baptized.' At Banyuls-sur-Mer (Pyrenées-Orientales) in 1883 the anti-clerical *patron* of a newly launched boat named *'Libre Penseur'* finally had to get a priest to bless her with the customary ceremonial, because he had been unable to persuade any man to go to sea in her.[8] In 1880 there was a fisherman at Saint-Cast on the North Coast of Brittany who caught very little fish in his new boat, and everybody was convinced that there must have been something wrong with her 'baptism.' The same belief was common in Normandy. Stories were told of many cases where boats had been lost at sea and their crews drowned because they had not been properly blessed by a priest. There was the saying:

> *Tout bateau qui n'est pas baptisé,*
> *Est conduit par le diable, et jeté sur les rochers.*[9]

It was the usual custom on the north coast of Brittany for the solemn 'baptism' of a new fishing boat to be postponed until three days after she had been brought to her home-port from where she had been built. Very often the ceremony took place on a Sunday. She was gaily decorated with flags and candles. After she had been named by the priest, one of the crew distributed *'pain bénit'* to the assistants, just as is done in French churches during Mass. Broken biscuits were scattered over the deck, then the skipper knocked a bottle of wine on the bows, saying:

> *Biscuit et bouteille de vin,*
> *Fais que sur mon bateau de manque jamais de pain.*

The 'godfather' and 'godmother' gathered up the biscuit crumbs and licked the drops of wine on the deck. The ceremony ended, a rope was tied round the skipper and his wife led him away like a sheep. For some mysterious reason he had to go to bed without any supper.

At Plouëzec, near Paimpol, the priest used to bless big round flat cakes, which were distributed in small pieces to those who had assisted at the blessing of a new fishing vessel. The ceremony began with the chanting of the *Te Deum*, after which the priest blessed the boat. Then the 'godfather' and 'godmother' each took a hammer and gave several blows on five small pegs, in the holes of which *pain-bénit* had been inserted. They formed a cross on the stern.

---

[8] P. Sébillot, in *Revue des Traditions populaires*, Vol. XIV, p. 394.
[9] P. Sébillot, *Le Folk-Lore des Pêcheurs*, p. 141.

The baptismal ceremonies ended with the singing of the *Ave Maris Stella;* after which the 'godfather' and 'godmother' distributed cakes and sugar-plums.[10]

Until fairly recent times the blessing of a new fishing vessel at Boulogne-sur-Mer was a very impressive function. The priest, vested in cotta and stole, accompanied the 'godfather' and 'godmother' to the boat building yard. All the men present took off their caps or hats, and everybody made the sign of the cross. The priest sprinkled every part of the vessel with holy water, starting at the stern. The crew looked on anxiously, lest he passed over even a few inches. Every bit of the rigging and tackle had to get a drop of holy water, otherwise damage was regarded as almost inevitable. After the final sign of the cross a maritime agape was served, with cakes and wine, not forgetting the sugar-plums provided by the 'godfather.' While this picnic was going on, one of the crew, laden with bottles, offered a drink to all those standing on the quay. It would bring bad luck if they refused. Lastly the 'godfather' and 'godmother' made an offering to the priest, and gave presents to each of the crew. At Boulogne it was not the custom to sing a canticle or hymn at the 'baptism' of a new fishing boat.[11]

On the North East Coast of Scotland a new boat was invariably launched to a flowing tide, but it did not matter whether her bow or stern entered the water first. On the other hand, there was the belief that it was unlucky to name her until she was afloat.[12] After this a bottle of whisky was broken over the bow or stern, according to which direction she had been launched. Bread and cheese, with whisky galore, were distributed to everybody present. Before breaking the bottle words like the following were recited:

> *Fae rocks an saands*
> *An barren lands*
> *An ill men's hands*
> *Keep's free.*
> *Weel oot, weel in,*
> *Wi a gweed shot.*

If a fishing boat had been built at another port, when she was

---

[10] ibid., pp. 143–4.

[11] cf. E. Deseille, *Glossaire du patois des matelots boulonnais* (Paris, 1884).

[12] It was the custom in some fisher communities when a boat 'was at her height,' i.e. fully planked, for her to be 'damped.' This meant that the shipwrights were treated to refreshments—lemonade, beer and, perhaps, whisky, with bread and cake.

berthed in her home port, it was sometimes the custom for the skipper's wife to take a lapful of corn or barley, and throw it over the boat. There was also the ritual in at least one village, the moment the bow touched the beach for the skipper to jump ashore, find the woman last married, take her arm, and drag her round the boat, even if this involved getting her legs wet. It was looked upon as a wise precaution to nail a horseshoe to the mast or any other part of a new boat.[13]

At Portessie, a fishing village east of Buckie, founded in 1727, and often known as Rottinsloch, men, women and children used to gather around a new boat when she was beached for the first time. It is related that one of them 'flang bere [barley] in ower the boat, sang oot the boat's name, and three cheer wiz gi'en.' [14] The barley was a sacrifice to the sea gods. Care had to be taken in choosing stones for ballast. In some fisher communities 'hunger steens,' i.e. those with holes in them, were looked upon as unlucky; in other places white stones.

Most if not all the traditional ritual and ceremonial connected with the building and launching of new boats on the East Coast of Scotland seems to have been of pagan origin. There is nothing about them which suggests that the skippers and crews professed any sort of Christianity. It has never been the custom for a Presbyterian minister to bless a new boat, or to offer prayer for the men who were to sail in her.

Even to-day Presbyterian owners and crews of new fishing vessels on the East Coast of Scotland appear to have greater faith in the quasi-sacramental virtues of unblessed whisky than in the 'Order for use at the launching of a ship' included in *Forms of Prayer for Use at Sea,* published by authority of the General Assembly about twenty-five years ago. This 'Order' is composed on traditional liturgical lines, having a certain affinity with the forms for the baptism of ships found in most Catholic rituals at least since the time of the Crusades, except for the sprinkling of the new vessel with holy water.[15]

---

[13] Horseshoes are regarded as protective amulets in almost every country where horses are shod; partly because they are made of iron, and partly because of the lunar symbolism, the shape being that of a horned new moon.

[14] W. Gregor, *Folk-Lore Journal,* Vol. IV, p. 11.

[15] It is curious that the 'Forms of Prayer to be used at sea,' inserted into the revised *Book of Common Prayer* in 1662, contain no prayers for blessing a ship. Neither does *The Scottish Book of Common Prayer* (1929), which ignores seafarers completely.

The 1925 edition of the *Rituale Romanum* includes two forms for bless-

At Ferryden, on the coast of Angus, and in other fishing villages, the 'christening' of a new boat with whisky usually led crews and their families to the nearest ale-house. The local schoolmaster, Andrew Douglas, writing in 1855, recalled that:

> 'when this event occurs information is given by the wife of the husband, or captain of the crew, as he is called. A good fresh skate, if procurable, is preferred, or, failing that, a large fresh cod, suitably boiled and served up, covered with butter and mustard, accompanied by a heap of potatoes, with their jackets on.
>
> 'The whole assembly set themselves to partake with great gusto —their knives and forks are their fingers and thumbs. The land-lord and landlady are sent for, and if any children or loungers are to be seen, all are pressed to sit down and take a share. . . . The conversation is all about the boat, and how she will sail. "Didna she look bonnie comin' doon the Stell the nicht! I'm sure Willie and oor Geordie gie'd 'er a guid trial." After healths have been drunk round, in all good feeling, and success to all the boats, a good winter or summer fishing, as the case may be, a song all round is called for. . . . Thus song, jibe, jeer and repartee, good-naturedly controlled, whiles away the evening till the clock strikes twelve "wi' an eerie croon." . . . On other occasions a dance forms the *finale*. A foursome reel takes place between the owner of the boat and mate, each taking the other's wife as partner, which, when performed in so spirited a manner, and so long sustained as to induce a due sense of fatigue, closes the scene. The company breaks up peaceably, and each "takes the road that suits himsel." ' [16]

In some fishing villages on the East Coast of Scotland it was the custom to allow a new boat to take the lead when leaving the beach or harbour for the first time. When the other boats hoisted their sails, and if there was not much of a breeze, the crews straining at their oars to overtake the new vessel. It was also an old tradition for the

---

ing ships. The *'benedictio solemnis navis piscatoris'* (approved by the S.R.C. in 1912) has a psalm, three collects, the first twenty-four verses of the twenty-first chapter of St. John's Gospel, and ends with the sprinkling of the vessel with holy water.

It would be interesting to know if the long 'Form of Prayer and Bene-diction when a Ship is about to depart from Port,' which finds a place in the Catholic Apostolic (Irvingite) *Liturgy and other Divine Offices of the Church*, was ever used for a fishing vessel before the last priest of this nineteenth century sect died. There is a rubric stating that he must be 'pro-perly vested.'

[16] *History of the Village of Ferryden* (2nd ed. Montrose, 1857), pp. 50–2.

owner's wife to give bread and cheese to the crews of all the other boats which arrived back from the fishing grounds after it. There is a story that there were occasions when a new boat remained at sea until the rest had returned and thus saved spending money on bread and cheese.[17]

It is a fairly common superstition that to change the name of a vessel will bring bad luck. Sir Charles Igglesden tells the story of how he asked an old fisherman at Folkestone what was the reason for a badly damaged boat lying on the beach, with a hole in her bottom. While chewing tobacco, the fisherman gave the following explanation:

> ' "It were like this. Bill's first wife were named Bertha, and this 'ere boat were named *Bertha*—and quite right, too. But she died last year, and Bill married agin—quite right, too—but damned if 'e don't go and re-christen the boat *Beatrice*, 'cause that were the name of 'is fresh wife. It's all wrong—agin Providence—for ain't it true that you must never rename a boat or a ship? 'E tempted Providence, and e's boat's smashed—and"— here the speaker's voice dropped to a low tone—"'e's smashed in more way nor one. That new wife's something tragic, a she-devil. Get a new boat by all means, but never change the name of the old 'un. Bill knows now—too late".' [18]

If a new boat on North Coast of Brittany was damaged or caught no fish on her first trip, it was usual for her to be laid up for a week. Only then would the skipper and crew venture to sea again.[19]

Scots fishermen until fairly recent times were so convinced that the spirits of the waves and the sea gods must have their prey that, not only were they afraid to save any one from drowning, but they dared not repair a boat of their own locality which had been wrecked with the loss of life and cast ashore. Mr. Gregor recalled that on the Buchan coast of Aberdeenshire about a hundred years ago:

> 'A fisherman of the village to which the boat belonged would not have set a foot in it to put to sea, and a board of it would not have been carried away as firewood by any of the inhabitants of the village. The boat was at times sold to a fisherman of another village, repaired, and did service for many a year.' [20]

---

[17] W. Gregor, op. cit., p. 197.
[18] *Those Superstitions* (1932), pp. 117–19.
[19] cf. P. Sébillot, op. cit., p. 148.
[20] *Notes on the Folk-Lore of the North-East of Scotland*, p. 198.

G

How deeply rooted was this superstition is shown by the following story. A fishing boat ran ashore at Collieston, with little damage done, but those who boarded her were drowned. Their friends refused to have anything more to do with the vessel, and would not sell her, for they were afraid to handle the money paid for a boat which had demanded the sacrifice of human lives.[21]

Just as fishermen in most parts of Europe were very particular about the fashion, cut and colour of their clothes until modern times, so were they even as conservative in the colours used on their vessels, which were painted according to traditions handed down from one generation to another. The selection of colours varied, so it was easy to tell at a glance the district to which a vessel belonged, even if her lines were no different to those of other boats in a harbour.

Until early in the nineteenth century most fishing vessels around the coast of Scotland were tarred, except the Shetland 'fourareens,' which, in keeping with Viking tradition, were often gaily painted. Both the North and South Isles Orkney boats had black or green bottoms, with white topsides. The earlier two-masted 'skaffies' on both sides of the Moray Firth had dark varnished topsides, with blue, white or green steerstrike, and blue or white gunwhales. Both the later and larger 'fifies' and 'zulus' displayed bright patches of colour on their deck-fittings, which contrasted with their usually black hulls. As time went on the boats' registered numbers and names on both bows and sterns became more and more ornate, the white paint picked out with blue, red, green, or even gold-leaf.

During the first decade of this century the steam-drifters belonging to ports on the East Coast of Scotland were the most gorgeously painted fishing vessels in Northern Europe. Their colour-schemes had been evolved from those of the sail-boats which preceded them. Every combination of colour was used, but reds, blues and greens predominated, making a contrast to black hulls. Some ports, however, fancied green or red hulls. The imitation graining on wheel-houses could only be done by a craftsman, for it was so realistic. Gold-leaf was sometimes used for details of funnels, capstans, ventilator cowls and mast-tops. Many a family-owned drifter displayed a metal shield on her funnel, with a heraldic device, a flower, or even a decorative landscape associated with her name. Masonic emblems sometimes mingled with elaborate scrowls on bows. The big white Roman letters and numbers painted on the bows and sterns of these proud little vessels were usually picked out with red, blue or green.

21 cf. Sébillot, op. cit., p. 149.

In Catholic countries superstition encouraged the use of Christian symbolism in the painting of fishing vessels, although in some cases it was mixed up with pagan emblems. But what must be stressed is that all this love of colour was bound up indirectly with folk-lore. It had its counterpart in the extravagantly painted horse-drawn wagons which were the homes of gypsies, or the merry-go-rounds at fairs.

Chapter Seven

TABOOS AND SUPERSTITIONS CONNECTED
WITH LIFE ASHORE

ONCE a new boat had been built, launched and blessed according
to some traditional rite, Christian or pagan, the crew had to be
careful to avoid doing all sorts of things which might bring them
bad luck. This also included not using certain words, or mentioning
specific objects.

On the North East Coast of Scotland fishermen would not pro-
nounce certain family names, especially Ross. It was also risky to
mention anybody of the name of Coull.[1] At Buckie, Banffshire, it
was formerly the custom to speak of 'spitting out the bad name.'
If either of these two surnames was spoken everybody present had
to spit, i.e. 'chiff.' A person bearing a 'bad name' was known as a
'chiffer-oot.' The only way to get round the difficulty was by circumlocution. For instance, one could say: 'The man it diz so in so,'
or 'The lad as lives at sic an' sic a place,' or just use the 'Tee-
name.' When men from the Highlands were hired before the herring
seasons, as was the custom in olden times, it was better to avoid
one with the name of Ross. There are stories of men with 'bad
names' having been hired before their names were known, who
were refused wages at the close of the season if the fishing had been
bad. The bad luck was attributed to their presence on board.

There also existed the fear of lodging in a house whose owner
bore a 'bad name.' Mr. Gregor relates that during the 1860s or
early 1870s a woman said to a drifter-skipper's daughter at Peterhead: 'Ye hanna hid sic a fishin this year as ye hid the last.' The
lassie replied: 'Na, na; faht wye cud we? Ye needna speer faht
wye we cudna. We wiz in a "chiffer-oot's" 'oose; we cudna hae
a fishin.'

The skipper's daughter, who had been taking her share in the
cutting, salting and packing of the herring, had lodged with a
family named Ross.[2]

In some villages on the East Coast of Aberdeenshire fishermen
regarded it was most unlucky if they met anybody named Whyte on

[1] Other surnames ending with double consonants, e.g. Campbell, were
looked upon as unlucky, and 'chiffed oot.' At Cullen, both 'Anderson' and
'Duffus' were regarded as evil names. Any one with the former name was
referred to as 'the man who sells the coals.'
[2] *Notes on the Folk-Lore of the North-East of Scotland*, p. 201.

their way to their boats, or on any other occasion. They were sure that their lines would be lost, or that very little fish would be caught.[3]

At Eyemouth, Berwickshire, the fishermen had an equal fear of using the word 'salt.' There is a story that in 1905 an Eyemouth drifter ran short of salt when engaged in herring fishing. So he hailed a Yarmouth drifter, and said: 'We need something we dinna want tae speak aboot.' The English skipper shouted back: 'Is it salt you want?' The salt was handed over, but all the Scots crew had disappeared below rather than hear the terrible word spoken in their presence.[4]

A fisherman making his way to the harbour or beach where his boat was berthed was like a sailor trying to navigate between the two rocks, Scylla and Charybdis, and the whirlpool in the Straits of Messina, where in the days of sail it was hard to steer clear of the one without being caught by the other.[5] There were so many human beings and animals which had to be given a wide berth. First of all there were men and women with unlucky names. Next came people with red hair or flat feet, but in this case their evil influence could be averted if one was quick enough to speak to them first. At Portknockie, Banffshire, and probably in other ports on the North East Coast of Scotland, dogs were looked upon as 'ill-fitted.'[6] Stories are told there of more than one who met a dog when going down to the harbour below the cliffs, pursued and killed it, for fear that the same animal might cross his path another morning. But to have encountered a hare or a rabbit was much worse. If a fisherman should meet a minister on his way to the boat, that again was more than enough to cause the whole crew to remain ashore for the day; though there was the superstition that the sinister effects of the Calvinist religion he propagated could be diverted by a timely appeal to 'cauld iron.'

Most Yorkshire fishermen had a horror of seeing any drowned animal on the shore or in the harbour when they were on the way to their boats. It was quite enough to stop them from going to sea.

---

[3] ibid., p. 201.

[4] cf. P. F. Anson, *Fishing Boats and Fisher Folk on the East Coast of Scotland* (1930), p. 38. There are countless superstitions connected with salt, which is usually regarded as bringing good luck (cf. E. and M. Radford, *Encyclopedia of Superstitions*, rev. ed. 1961, p. 297).

[5] See Homer, *Odyssey*, XII.

[6] For some mysterious reason it was regarded as unlucky to ask a Moray Firth fisherman for the loan of anything on a Monday, but he did not mind borrowing from another person who had the reputation of being 'lucky.' Forty years ago if one asked a match from a fisherman, more likely than not he broke a bit off the end, for fear of losing his luck.

Again, it was an insult to ask a fisherman about to put to sea where he intended to shoot his lines or nets. For this was regarded as certain to bring bad luck. It would have been quite correct for him to have answered: 'Deel cut oot yer ill tongue.' Incidentally, the word 'kirk' could never be used, and this presented difficulties, because churches often served as landmarks at sea. All one could do was to refer to them as a 'bell-hoose.' If there was any reason to speak of a minister, once again circumlocution had to be adopted by calling him, e.g. 'the man wi' the black quyte (coat).'

At Eyemouth, Berwickshire, on more than one occasion, so it is related, the fishermen were greatly alarmed when sheep and pigs were washed down into the harbour when the Eye Water was in spate. Stories were told on more than one part of the coast of boys getting hold of rabbit skins, filling them with rubbish, and placing them in the sterns of boats to stop the crews from going to sea. Cats were regarded as lucky in most fisher communities. J. B. B. Baker relates in his *History of Scarborough* (1882) that almost every fisherman's wife kept a black cat in the belief that the animal would bring her husband back from sea. 'This gave black cats such a value that no one else could keep them; they were always stolen.'

The pig taboo, so certain folk-lore historians have stated, may have been carried to Scotland across the North Sea by Celtic intruders from the Continent in remote times.[7] Dean Ramsay (1793–1872) has a story in his *Reminiscences of Scottish Life and Character*, which deals with a fishing village on the coast of Fife, but what is related might have occurred in almost any fisher community. The parish minister invited a friend to conduct the Sunday morning service, having failed to convince him of the universal pig taboo.

'It was arranged that his friend was to read the chapter relating to the herd of swine into which the evil spirits were cast. Accordingly, when the first verse was read in which the unclean beast was mentioned, a slight commotion was observed among the audience, each one of them putting his or her hand on any piece of iron—a nail on the seat or bookboard, or to the nails on their shoes. At the repetition of the word again and again, more commotion was visible, and the words "cauld airn" (cold iron), the antidote to this baneful spell, were heard issuing from various corners of the church. And finally, on his coming over the hated

[7] cf. D. A. Mackenzie, *Scottish Folk-Lore and Folk Life* (1935), Chapter II, 'Swine Cults: Sanctity and Abhorrence of Pig.'

word again, when the whole herd ran violently down the bank into the sea, the alarmed parishioners, irritated beyond bounds, rose and all left the church in bodies.' [8]

There was a similar fear of swine on the coast of Angus. The fisher folk at Arbroath and Auchmithie

'had a great aversion to the flesh of the pig coming into contact with their boats. If any evil-disposed person had managed surreptitiously to place a piece of pork on board a boat before its leaving the harbour on a fishing expedition, although its presence had not been discovered till the boat had reached the fishing ground, those on board would return to the land without shooting their nets rather than proceed with their fishing with the hated junk aboard.' [9]

Some Scottish superstitions and taboos existed among English and French fishermen, and those of certain other European countries. Not only on the Channel coasts of England, Normandy and Brittany, but also in Sweden, it was regarded as unlucky for a fisherman to be asked where he was going when on his way to his boat. At Saint-Malo and other Breton ports, it was a worse portent if the inquirer happened to be a woman. Swedish fishermen, as well as French ones on the Bay of Biscay and Mediterranean coasts, dreaded being wished 'good luck' before putting to sea. It was all right however if one said a prayer for them, e.g. *'Dieu t'en envoie!'* [10] Fishermen on the Côtes-du-Nord used to believe that if anybody stared at them when they were making for their boats, it would bring bad luck.

In the villages between Paimpol and Tréguier—a district always full of superstitions—no fisherman in olden times would have dared to go to sea if he chanced to meet a tailor; though some believed that his 'evil eye' could be averted by a prayer to Our Lady. Tailors were also feared in certain places on the South Coast of Brittany, and it was dangerous to mention one by name before boarding a fishing boat.[11]

It should be mentioned that all seafarers have believed it to be unlucky to meet a clergyman of any Christian denomination when

[8] *Scottish Religious Feelings and Observances*, Chapter II, 22nd ed., 1872.
[9] J. M. McBain, *Arbroath: Past and Present* (Arbroath, 1887), pp. 75–6.
[10] W. Jones, *Credulities, Past and Present* (1880), p. 116; *Revue des Traditions populaires*, Vol. VI, p. 117; Vol. IX, p. 219.
[11] *Revue des Traditions populaires*, Vol. VI, p. 541.

on their way to their vessels, or to see one standing near them. This is an ancient and almost universal superstition. It is possible that it arose in the early days of Christianity, when a sailor acknowledged Christ ashore, but put greater faith in his old gods when he was afloat. It does not appear to be associated with any anti-clerical feeling; and it may have its origins in far off times when whatever was holy or consecrated was looked upon as a centre of either malignant or beneficial power, outside the control of ordinary human beings.[12] Thus most Catholic fishermen have had the same fear of meeting priests as Protestant ones had of their ministers.

Around Paimpol, if a fisherman on his way to his boat chanced to meet a *dévote*, that is a woman known for her piety, he returned home, took holy water, recited an Our Father and Hail Mary, and made the sign of the cross. Only then would he dare to go to sea.[13] On the North Coast of Brittany there existed a widespread fear of meeting a nun before embarking, for she was thought to be as unlucky as a priest. Cats were put into the same class, above all if encountered after dark.[14] On the other hand to meet a horse or a donkey was a good omen.

Another very common superstition among Protestant fishermen was the fear of meeting a woman—even wives—on their way to their boats. It existed in Cornwall, on the Isle of Lewis in the Outer Hebrides, and in Yorkshire. At Staithes, a village north of Whitby, the women used to turn their backs on the fishermen when they saw them going down the steep street to the little harbour where their cobles were berthed.[15] Both in Scotland and in Sweden it was regarded as most unlucky for a woman to walk over a fishing line.[16]

Hares were specially dreaded by both fishermen and farmers, because it was believed that a witch often turned herself into a hare to perform evil deeds.[17] If a hare, or any part of a hare, was found in a boat or a fish-wife's creel, it was a sure sign of some great misfortune about to happen.[18] Hares were feared on certain parts of the coast of Brittany just as much as they were in almost every fisher community on the East Coast of Scotland, likewise in Cornwall. No doubt the fisher folk at Nairn recalled that in 1662, Isobel

---

[12] cf. Radford, *Encyclopedia of Superstitions*, p. 104.
[13] P. Sébillot, op. cit., p. 183.
[14] cf. this with the Yorkshire belief that cats, especially black ones, brought good luck (see pp. 104, 131, 137).
[15] ibid., p. 184.
[16] *Folk-Lore Journal*, Vol. I, p. 355.
[17] Rabbits were also feared, though not so much as hares (see p. 105).
[18] Gregor, op. cit., p. 129.

Gowdie, the famous witch who lived only two-and-a-half miles away at Auldearn, confessed:

> *I shall go intill a hare,*
> *With sorrow and sych and meikle care;*
> *And I shall go in the Devil's name*
> *Ay while I come home again.*

When she wanted to resume human form she repeated:

> *Hare, hare, God send thee care.*
> *I am in a hare's likeness just now,*
> *But I shall be in a woman's likeness even now.*[19]

Dougal Graham relates in his chap-book, *The History of Buckhaven,* how great was the fear of 'maukins' (hares) among the fisher folk:

'None will go down to the sea that day when they see a maukin, or if a wretched body put in a maukin's fit in their creels, they need not lift them that day, as it will be bad luck, either broken backs, or legs, or arms, or hear bad accounts of the boats at sea.' [20]

He also tells us that

'the laddies and lassies when they go to gather bait tell strange stories about witches, ghosts, willy-with-the-wisp, and the Kelpy, Fairies, Maukins, and boggles of all sorts. . . . The ghosts, like old horses, go all night for fear they are seen, and be made to carry skate, or to be carried, and witches are the worst kind of devils, and make use of cats to ride on, or kill-kebbers [kiln-rafters] and besoms [brooms], and sail over seas in cockle shells, and witch lads and lassies and disable others.'

'Willy-o'-the-Wisp' was specially dreaded by the fisher lads and lassies in this village on the coast of Fife, because he was

'the fiery devil, who leads people off their road to drown them, for he speaks sometimes at our feet, and then turns before us with his candle, as if he were two or three miles before us. Many a good boat has Spunkie drown'd; the boats coming to land in the night time, they observe a light off the land, and set upon it and drown.'

[19] cf. J. M. McPherson, op. cit., p. 164.
[20] op. cit., pp. 135–6.

Also greatly feared was the Kelpie, i.e. the water-horse, described by Dougal Graham as 'a sly devil, who roars before a loss at sea, and frightens both old and young upon the shore.' It seems that the kelpie was usually a black horse with staring eyes, though sometimes he was white. More rarely he assumed the form of a man, and as such tried to make love to a woman. Alternatively the water spirit took female form and was known as the water wraith.

A few more superstitions associated with going to sea are worth mentioning. On the Isle of Guernsey, the sound of a cock crowing at an unusual hour was regarded as unlucky, just as it was on the North East Coast of Scotland.[21] On the Yorkshire coast, if a fisherman sent his son to look for his sea-boots; the latter had to carry them under his arms; if he rested them on his shoulders, quite likely the father would refuse to embark that morning.[22] At Scarborough there was the superstition that if a china bowl had been turned upside down, it was a warning not to go to sea.[23]

The presence of a dove or a pigeon on a boat was quite enough to stop any fisherman on the East Coast of Scotland from putting to sea; in spite of the fact that a dove was usually an emblem of all that was good. Andrew Douglas, the schoolmaster at Ferryden, told the story of a boat's crew that returned early one morning from sea, without shooting their lines; merely because an exhausted pigeon, pursued by a hawk, had taken refuge in the boat. He tried to convince them of their folly, but one of the men turned to him and said impatiently: 'It's easy for you to speak there; but, had we no turned in time, ye'd ne'er seen helt nor hair o' our boat's lines; we'd been i' the boddom o' the sea, an' God kens far. Slag, dash oot the brains o't! It's been lang eneuch glow'ring i' our face!' Having killed the pigeon, one of the crew hurried to the nearest alehouse for half a gill of whisky; his last words to the schoolmaster being: 'Gude keep's a' frae seein' unearthly sights—they're nae couthie.'[24]

Here are two more stories about men alleged to be 'ill-fitted.' In one village there were a pair of them. Each knew his neighbour's bad reputation, but he did not know his own. One morning both got out of bed early to look at the sky. They met each other, took fright, and each went back to his house. The result was that the village lost a day's fishing.

The boats of two villages were together one afternoon during

[21] cf. Victor Hugo, *Les Travailleurs de la mer.*
[22] P. Sébillot, op. cit., p. 190.
[23] W. Jones, op. cit., p. 115.
[24] op. cit., p. 16.

the summer herring season, waiting for the time to put to sea. Mr. Gregor relates that:

> 'One of the boats outside belonged to a man who was reputed to have an "ill-fit." When he came to go on board his boat, he had to step across another boat or two. When he put his foot on the boat nearest the shore he was met with an oath and the words, "Keep aff o' ma boat, ye hiv an ill fit." The man drew back quickly, and turned to the master of the next boat, and, addressing him by his "tee name," said "F—, a'm sure ye'll lat me o'er your boat." Permission was readily granted. The boats put to sea. The only herrings brought ashore were in F—'s boat; and it was the man with the "ill-fit" that gave them.' [25]

The average fisherman in almost every country in Europe until about a hundred years ago, no matter whether he regarded himself as a Papist, Protestant, or pagan, seldom forgot the warning given by St. Peter the Fisherman in his First Epistle 'to the elect who dwell as foreigners up and down Pontus, Galatia, Cappadocia, Asia, and Bithynia,' when he wrote:

> 'Be sober, and watch well; the devil, who is your enemy, goes about roaring like a lion, to find his prey.'

Even if fishermen and fisher lads were not always sober when they were ashore, and not often well grounded in their faith, they did watch and face the devil boldly in whatever form he chose to take. There were more things than those already recalled in this chapter which must be done or not done before putting to sea. Some were connected with portents of good or bad fishing, others with favourable or unfavourable days or seasons of the year.

Along the Bay of Biscay, the Breton fishermen knew for certain that if the wind blew from a westerly direction during the Gospel of the Mass on Palm Sunday, they would have no luck the next time they shot nets for herring. They prayed for a north or south-east wind. Early in the last century fisher folk on the North East Coast of Scotland hoped for a westerly wind on New Year's Eve, for this was a good omen.[26]

[25] op. cit., pp. 198–9.
[26] G. de la Landelle, *Moeurs maritimes* (Paris, 1867), p. 143. At Portessie the swell before a storm was known as the 'win' chap.' In this same Banff-shire village the old folk used to say that the sea before any disaster from drowning had 'a waichty melody,' or 'a death groan.' At Buckie 'the win' chap' or buffet before a storm was also called 'the dug afore its maister.'

When porpoises were seen off the north coast of Brittany, every fisherman rejoiced. Most seamen regarded porpoises as lucky, and it was unwise to capture them. If they played around a vessel at sea, it was a good omen for the voyage. East Anglian fishermen used to say that if a porpoise was seen swimming swiftly northwards, it was a sign of fine weather, if southwards, of a gale.[27]

There were curious superstitions in some countries connected with the 'King Fish' of various species. The Breton fishermen believed that the sardines had their king, and if they found an exceptionally large sardine, the shoals would disappear sooner or later.[28] Sussex fishermen gave the name of 'king of the herrings' to a large blood-coloured herring, which swam like a pilot before a shoal of fish. If by chance he was caught in the meshes of their nets, he was thrown back into the sea; otherwise they could be sure of bad luck.[29] On the French Riviera there was a similar fear of catching a *'charran' (Serranus argus)*, for this species of fish, which lives in deep waters, was regarded as the portent of a tempest.[30] If squids appeared in the Bay of Biscay, fishermen on the coast of Asturias, dared not put to sea, because they knew there would be bad weather.[31]

There also existed a fear of the 'King of the Herrings' on the North Sea as well as on the English Channel, and fishermen used to say: 'Bad luck to him who has caught the King of the Herrings!' [32] Equally unlucky was a very large whiting; a sure portent that the catcher would be drowned sooner or later.

Fishermen on the East Coast of Scotland used to maintain that a late harvest betokened a late herring fishing.[33] If no cuttle-fish appeared off the Ile-de-Noirmoutier in the Bay of Biscay by a certain date, the farmers had little doubt of a bad harvest.[34]

The Channel Islands fishermen used to believe in the existence of a fish—actually a species of merman—whom they called 'King of the Auxcriniers,' much more unlucky than the 'King of the Herring.' Victor Hugo relates:

'He is small, in fact a dwarf. The names of all who have been drowned and the spots where they lie are well known to

[27] E. and M. A. Radford, *Encyclopedia of Superstitions*, p. 271.
[28] Cambry, *Voyage dans le Finistère*, p. 335.
[29] F. Sawyer, *Sussex Natural History, Folk-Lore and Superstitions* (Brighton, 1883), p. 12.
[30] J. B. Andrews, in *Revue des Traditions populaires*, Vol. IX, p. 219.
[31] Braulio Vigon, *Folk-Lore de la Mar*, p. 11.
[32] de la Landelle, op. cit., p. 122.
[33] Gregor, op. cit., p. 145.
[34] cf. P. Sébillot, op. cit., p. 154.

him. He has a deep knowledge of that great grave-yard which extends far and wide beneath the waters of the deep. His head is massive in the lower part and narrow in the forehead; his squat and corpulent figure; his skull, covered with wary excrescences; long legs, long arms, fins for feet, claws for hands, and a sea-green countenance; these are the characteristics of this king of the waves. Imagine a spectral fish with the face of a man. Nothing is more terrible than an interview with this monster: amid the rolling waves, or in the thick of the mist, the sailor sees sometimes a strange creature with wide nostrils, flattened ears, an enormous mouth, gap-toothed jaws, and large glaring eyes. In the livid lightning he appears red; when it is purple, he looks wan. He has a stiff spreading beard, running with water, and overlapping a sort of pelerine, ornamented with fourteen shells, seven before and seven behind. These shells are curious to those who are learned in conchology. The King of the Auxcriniers is only seen in stormy seas. He is the terrible forerunner of the tempest. His form traces itself in the fog, in the squall, in the tempest of rain. Scales cover his sides like a vest. He rises above the waves which fly before the wind, twisting and curling like thin shavings which fly beneath the carpenter's plane. Then his hateful form issues from the foam, and if there should be on the horizon a vessel in distress, his face lights up with an evil smile, and he dances a terrible and uncouth dance. It is an omen of evil to meet him on a voyage.' [35]

Certain species of birds could portend good or bad luck at sea. In olden times fishermen at Dover and Folkestone, when they heard the cries of long-beaked curlews, which they called the 'Seven Whistlers,' were certain that they were an omen of death or shipwreck.[36] On the Côtes-du-Nord cormorants were feared, and when fishermen saw them they said:

> *Quand on les voit sur les rochers*
> *La marée est manqué.*

[35] *The Toilers of the Sea*, Book I, Chapter 4. In this novel we are told that the mysterious fisherman named Gilliatt, whom the people of Saint Sampson accused of indulging in every kind of superstitious practice, and who was said to have conversed with the King of the Auxcriniers, owned a shell taken off the skin of this sea-monster. Other men who alleged they had seen the King declared that he had only thirteen shells left on his body. Gilliatt was also reputed to a '*Marcou*,' i.e. the seventh male child born consecutively. Other folk were sure that he was a '*Cambion*,' with the devil for his father.

[36] W. Henderson, *Notes on the Folk-Lore of the Northern Counties* (1879), p. 131.

If they heard sea-gulls crying: 'Caré! Caré! Caré! ' it was a warning
to haul in the lines, or not to venture out to sea.[37] In many coastal
areas of Europe sea-gulls were, and still are, believed to embody the
souls of dead fishermen and sailors, especially those drowned at sea.
For this reason they must never be killed, and it is an act of charity
to feed them, even if they are cruel and greedy.

Swallows were usually regarded as good omens when they darted
over the sea, above all during the summer mackerel season. When
fishermen at Dover and Folkestone heard the sound of red-wings,
which they called 'Herring-Spear' or 'Herring-Piece,' as the birds
crossed the Channel in search of a warmer climate, they were afraid,
although it could portend a good fishing.[38]

No birds were more welcomed by the fishermen on the south
side of the Moray Firth than wild geese flying north. Then it was
safe to venture out to sea. At Lossiemouth and the adjacent villages
there was the rhyme:

> *Wild geese, wild geese, gangin t' the sea,*
> *Good weather it will be.*
> *Wild geese, wild geese, gangin t' the hill,*
> *The weather it will spill.*

Cuckoos were regarded by almost all fishermen as bringers of
good luck and good weather. At Saint-Jacut-de-la-Mer, on the
Côtes-du-Nord, it was believed that the cuckoo was specially partial to skate. The first boat that noticed the bird used to throw out
bits of this fish as a sacrificial offering; the crew then felt sure that
they would do well for the rest of the summer fishing season.[39]

When shoals of fish did not arrive at the usual time or disappeared suddenly, fisher folk generally attributed it to some
paranormal reason. Long ago at Tenby, South Wales, it was said
that the fish had swum away from the grounds on the Bristol
Channel, because of a crime committed in the town.[40] In 1886, there
was an equally strong conviction in at least one little village on
the coast of Morbihan that if the Republican government were
overthrown, the sardines could return in abundance, for at that time
there were only mackerel in the strait between the mainland and the
Ile-de-Groix.[41] At Étretat, the fisher folk used to say that after the
fall of Napoleon and his banishment to St. Helena, herring had
deserted the coasts of Normandy.[42]

[38] Henderson, op. cit., p. 131.
[39] P. Sébillot, op. cit., p. 157.
[40] W. Jones, *Credulities, Past and Present*, p. 113.
[41] *Le Temps*, April 23, 1886.
[42] A. Karr, *La Famille Alain*, p. 482.

On Belle-Ile, six miles from the coast of Morbihan, formerly very isolated from the rest of the world, there was a chapel dedicated to St. Joseph, to which the fishermen used to visit at the end of the season. One day a man took an image of St. Peter to the chapel, and shoved St. Joseph into a cave at the far end of the island. Not long after this a fisherman, returning from his boat, and going to pray in the chapel, beheld, not the statue of St. Joseph, but the carpenter of Nazareth in person. Standing beside him was a lady dressed in white, evidently the Virgin Mary, who was trying to console him. But it was clear that she had failed to do so, because the fisherman noticed a big tear on his cheek. According to the story, the sea became too salt with tears for the sardines to remain there, and they swam away from Belle-Ile.[43]

There were lucky and unlucky days to go fishing, when, even if the weather seemed fair, it would have been dangerous for a boat to venture out to sea. In most countries, as might be expected, fishermen remained ashore on Sundays. In certain Catholic communities it was permissible to start fishing on a Sunday afternoon, for this presumed that the crews had assisted at Mass. Stories have been handed down on the Côtes-du-Nord of what happened to fishermen who went to sea on a Sunday. At Saint-Cast and Saint-Jacut-de-la-Mer, *la Sainte Vierge* is said to have appeared in human form to register her protests. Divine wrath was apparent soon afterwards; several boats were lost; fish disappeared from the Banc de la Horaine, and the Devil took possession of it.[44]

The fishermen at Morrison's Haven, Prestonpans, during the eighteenth century revered Satan more than any saint, After their parish minister had prayed and protested against their sailing for the fishing grounds on the Firth of Forth before the Sabbath was past, it is recorded that 'to prevent any injury accruing from his prayers, they make a small image of rags and burn it on the top of their chimneys.' [45] Their object, so it seems, was to injure the minister by resorting to a common form of black magic.

On some parts of the coasts of Spain it was regarded as unlucky to go fishing on a Friday.[46] Far more dangerous was it to venture forth on Good Friday. There was a superstition around Paimpol, in Brittany, that if any man was guilty of profaning this day of mourning, instead of taking fish, he would suffer many crosses.[47]

---

[43] E. Herpin, in *Revue des traditions populaires*, Vol. XIII, p. 98.
[44] P. Sébillot, op. cit., p. 163.
[45] *Choice Notes from Notes and Queries—Folk-Lore* (1859), p. 271.
[46] Scottish fishermen on the Moray Firth Coast when barking nets before the herring season avoided Fridays as unlucky. As far as possible barking (tanning) always took place during the incoming tide.
[47] cf. Sébillot, op. cit., p. 165.

At Saint-Cast and other villages west of Saint-Malo, no fisherman would dare to go to sea on Easter Sunday, otherwise porpoises would drive mackerel away from the coast.

It was on Ascension Day one year that some fishermen at Saint-Cast, who had gone to sea despite the warnings of their *curé*, were confronted for the first time by the 'devil-fish' known as *'le gros Nicole,'* just as they were about to shoot their lines on the banc de la Horaine. Because St. Peter had been a fisherman, his feast day, June 29th, was observed as a day of rest in almost all fisher communities.

For different reasons it was safer not to shoot nets or lines on November 2nd, All Souls' Day. Quite likely human bones and skulls would be brought up instead of fish. Such was the belief on many parts of the Mediterranean coast of France, and it was the same at Dieppe.[48]

After the Reformation when Calvinism superseded Catholicism as the religion of the majority of the inhabitants of the Channel Islands, superstition increased among the fisher folk, although Victor Hugo wrote in 1866 that in bygone times the Roman Catholics of this archipelago 'were, in spite of themselves, in closer connection with Satanic influences than the Huguenots. Why this should have been the case we cannot say; but there can be no doubt that much annoyance was experienced by the minority, from this source. Satan had a weakness for the Catholics, which gave rise to the opinion that the Devil is more Catholic than Protestant.'[49]

There used to be a good fishery for herring at Guernsey until 1830, when it suddenly came to an end. It is related that:

'On the evening of Easter Day in that year some boats, contrary to the usual custom of not fishing on a Sunday, went out with their drift-nets in pursuit of the herrings, and succeeded in catching some thousands of these fish. The herrings were brought on shore and sold readily in the market; but as the fishermen were bringing their captures to the market-place they were met by an old man whose many years had been spent on the stormy seas which wash the rocky shores of the island, and who, throughout his long career, had been accustomed to regard Sunday as a day of rest alike for fishes and fishermen. He inquired of the fishermen, now heavily laden with their spoil, "When did you

---

[48] cf. P. Sébillot, op. cit., p. 166; and A. Bosquet, *La Normandie romanesque* (Paris, 1845), p. 276.
[49] *The Toilers of the Sea,* Book I, Chapter II.

catch these fish?" "Last night—Sunday night," was the reply. "Sunday night! " said he, "then we shall have no more herrings." There has been no herring fishery at Guernsey since that year.'[50]

Sunday fishing was the reason given by old men for the disappearance of herring off two ports on the East Coast of Scotland —Dunbar and Stonehaven. Both were prosperous to an extraordinary degree until about the middle of the last century, but the herring vanished one year and never returned.[51]

The Lutheran fishermen on the Baltic in olden times never shot their nets between All Saints' (November 1st) and St. Martin's Day (November 11th). They believed that this would bring them bad luck for the rest of the year.[52]

On the North West Coast of Spain, no fisherman dared to go to sea on July 25th, the feast of St. James the Apostle, whose relics are venerated in the Cathedral at Compostela.[53]

There were other saints' days observed in different ports that prevented fishing being done, too numerous to be mentioned in detail. So what with both pagan and Christian superstitions it is surprising that anybody had the courage to earn his living as a fisherman; such countless dangers faced him on all sides, most of them from invisible sources.

---

[50] E. W. H. Holdsworth, *Deep-Sea Fishing and Fishing Boats* (1874), p. 215.

[51] cf. P. F. Anson, *Fishing Boats and Fisher Folk on the East Coast of Scotland* (1930), p. 66.

[52] cf. P. Sébillot, op. cit., p. 168.

[53] cf. *Boletino folkorico espanolo*, p. 44.

H

Chapter Eight

TABOOS AND SUPERSTITIONS AT SEA

AT last we have got the fisherman ready to go to sea, but there were still omens and portents which might make him change his mind at the last moment. Most fisher communities used to have an old man who got up early in the morning to examine the sky, and prophesy the weather for the day. If he decided for various mysterious reasons that it looked good, he went round the village to awaken the crews.

Early in the last century there was a 'wise-man' at Ferryden, on the coast of Angus, with the name of James West, commonly known as 'Bull Waast.' It is recorded that:

'James was generally early abroad in the mornings, in order to discern the face of the sky. Many watched his motions; and if it was observed that he stood with his hands folded below his jacket, they would all turn into the beds again; but if the hands were placed behind his back, this was an omen to proceed to sea; and if James was observed drawing down his boat, there was a rush immediately, and cries of "Jamie, bring this, and Geordie, bring that," were heard on every side.' [1]

But it was not always safe to rely on human weather prophets, for as has been related in the previous chapter, many fishermen put greater faith in the flight and cries of certain birds. For instance, during the summer months, when shoals of mackerel could be expected off the Côtes-du-Nord, the fishermen at Saint-Cast kept their ears open for cuckoos. Then they lit their clay pipes, as if to offer incense to the birds, and said:

Quand le cocou chante avant que nous soyons embarqués;
Les maquereaux sont en route pour venir nous trouver.

On the other hand, if they heard the cuckoo before they had eaten anything, they recited the verse:

[1] Andrew Douglas, *History of the Village of Ferryden* (2nd ed. Montrose, 1857), p. 13.

Nous ne pouvons nous en aller;
Car nous sommes bien faînés (fascinés)
Nous avons ouï le parent chanter
Et nous n'avons pas dejeuné.[2]

On the north coast of Brittany it was the custom for the skipper to rouse the crew from their box-beds. He knocked at each door and shouted:

Debout, matelots,
Les autres bateaux
Sont déjà partis pour les Bourdineaux.

This was one of the favourite fishing grounds off Saint-Cast. Before the fishermen at this Breton port hoisted the sails of their boats, they partook of a ceremonial drink of brandy, which they called *'boire la goutte.'* They maintained that the fish smelt the drink, and were attracted by it to the lines or nets. Whenever there was a good price for the day's catch, the crew always expected a bottle of brandy to be given them.[3]

On certain parts of the East Coast of Scotland there was the superstition of throwing a handful of salt behind the skipper when the fishing was poor. Otherwise one of the crew cast salt over the boat by way of a blessing.[4]

The cod-fishermen on the Newfoundland Banks, as well as those in some ports in Brittany and Normandy, used to have a super-stitious respect for what they called the *'os de verité.'* These are two bones near the gills of a cod which resemble turned-back blades. Various curious rites were performed with them. According to the sound made when dropped or when hit, the *'os de verité'* answered 'yes' or 'no.' Two hard parts on the head of a skate were consulted in the same manner.[5]

Before the start of the mackerel season at the end of April it was the custom at Brighton to decorate the masts of the tubby little boats with garlands of flowers. Bread and cheese, which played such an important part in fisher superstitions elsewhere, were

---

[2] P. Sébillot, op. cit., p. 189. The fishermen called the cuckoo 'le parent.' In most parts of Europe there were omens in relation to the first call of the cuckoo.
[3] P. Sébillot, op. cit., pp. 171–2.
[4] W. Gregor, in *Folk-Lore Journal*, Vol. III, p. 309.
[5] P. Sébillot, *Traditions et superstitions de la Haute-Bretagne* (Paris, 1882), Vol. II, pp. 263–4.

distributed to children on the shingly beach, who wished the boats good luck.[6]

All sorts of persons and objects were regarded as unlucky on board a fishing vessel when their crews were more credulous than they are to-day. Strange as it seems, husbands of unfaithful wives, otherwise cuckolds, were looked upon as lucky on the North Coast of Brittany, where there was the saying: *'Chanceux comme un cocu.'* It was the same at Boulogne-sur-Mer at one time. If a boat caught plenty of turbot, the crew would be sure that the wife of one of them must have slept with another man.[7] The belief went even further on the Côtes-du-Nord, where bawdy jokes were passed if a boat was exceptionally lucky, for this was attributed to one of the crew having slept with the *patron's* wife the night before going to sea.[8]

No fisherman at Audierne would go to sea if he found a cat on board his boat. If a Scots fisherman discovered a rat, he had to kill it, so that the blood spilt would avert the spell cast.[9] Around the Bay of Saint-Malo there was a general belief that fishing boats must not be kept too clean, otherwise fish would not come near them, for they were attracted by the smell of rotten guts. On the *terre-neuvas* there was a ritual dirtiness, so that the cod would be lured towards the vessels by the powerful odour wafted over the water.[10] The same superstition existed on the East Coast of Scotland, where it was believed that herring scales ought not to be washed off the decks of the sailing drifters.[11] Some Breton fishermen were sure that nothing brought better luck to a boat than a rotting octopus. It was kept for a week, then cut up, and the putrified bits scattered over and into every corner of the boat. One fisherman at Saint-Cast had such a faith in the magic powers of an octopus that he never went to sea without a dead one in the bottom of his boat.

Scots fishermen often trusted to twigs of rowan-trees to keep away fairies, and sometimes tied them to their lines and the thole-

---

[6] F. Sawyer, *Sussex Folk-Lore*, p. 4. At Looe, and other places in Cornwall, there was the belief that before a great catch of pilchards a noise like stones rolling was heard in the cellars where the fish were packed. People would say that the piskies were truckling the pressing-stones, i.e. the flat stones by which the pilchards were compressed into the barrels (see R. Thurston Hopkins, *Small Sailing-Craft* (1931), p. 220).

[7] cf. E. Deseille, *Glossaire Boulonnais.*

[8] cf. Sébillot, op. cit., p. 194.

[9] W. Gregor, in *Folk-Lore Journal*, Vol. IV, p. 14.

[10] P. Sébillot, *Traditions et superstitions de la Haute-Bretagne*, Vol. II, p. 247.

[11] W. Gregor, in *Folk-Lore Journal*, Vol. II, p. 308.

pins for their oars.[12] This is not surprising, for the rowan, or moun-
tain-ash, was credited almost everywhere with the power of averting
witchcraft, disease, and the Evil Eye. As stated already, horseshoes were often nailed to the masts of Scottish fishing vessels.
Although the majority of Boulogne fishermen were pious Catholics,
this did not prevent them from believing in many curious superstitions. One was that a boat was sure to have bad luck if some
object fell into the water as she was leaving port.[13] Some fishermen
on the Buchan coast of Aberdeenshire, if they formed the opinion
that a boat was bewitched, would not dare to go to sea until a net
had been burned as a sacrifice to the evil spirit.[14] Breton fishermen
shared this belief in the efficacy of fire for driving the devil out of a
boat.[15]

It was the custom in most countries of Northern Europe for the
crew of a fishing boat to offer prayer once they got away from shore,
for reasons that were usually superstitious. Even the Lutheran
fishermen on the isle of Gotland in the Baltic used to make the sign
of the cross. So did the Iceland crews early in the nineteenth century.[16] On the North Coast of Spain, when a fishing boat left the
harbour, the skipper took off his cap, and holding the tiller, said a
prayer asking for a blessing on the fishing.[17]

A hundred years ago, when the fishermen at Dieppe were better
Catholics than they are to-day, it was the custom for daily prayers
to be said in common on *chasse-marées* and luggers when
they were at sea. The ceremonial accompanying this maritime
worship was quite elaborate, and to omit any detail was regarded
as sure to bring bad luck. First it was the duty of a *mousse* to call
the crew with this invitation to prayer:

> *A la prière,*
> *Devant et arrière,*
> *Depuis l'étrave jusqu'à l'étambord*
> *Réveille qui dort.*

While the rest of the crew were getting out of their bunks, the
mousse lit what was called *'la chandelle du bon Dieu,* and said
aloud:

---

[12] W. Gregor, *Further Report on Folk-Lore in Scotland* (Toronto, 1897),
pp. 475, 487.
[13] cf. Sébillot, op. cit., p. 199.
[14] W. Gregor, in *Folk-Lore Journal,* Vol. III, p. 308.
[15] H. le Carguet, in *Revue des traditions populaires,* Vol. IV, p. 537.
[16] F. S. Bassett, *Legends of the Sea,* p. 387.
[17] B. Vigon, *Folk-lore de la Mar,* p. 15.

La chandelle du bon Dieu est allumée
Au saint nom de Dieu soit alizée,
Au profit du maître et de l'équipage
Bon temps, bon vent, pour conduire la barque,
Si Dieu plait.

After this one of the older fishermen, known as the *curé*, recited certain prayers. On Sundays and feast-days bits of the Mass and Vespers which the men knew by heart were added, although many of them were unable to read.[18]

On the big Boulogne ketches, with crews of at least sixteen men, or on the smaller luggers, the skipper recited the following grace before meals:

Os allons faire au nom du Père
Avant d'aller à l'caudière.[19]

It is recorded that early in the last century fishermen on the island of Sardinia were equally pious, for the skippers used to chant or recite litanies of Our Lady and the Saints, with the crew responding *Ora pro nobis*. Then followed a sort of ritual changing into old clothes. St. Peter, St. Anthony of Padua and St. Michael were always invoked at sea, because they were supposed to take a special interest in fishermen.[20]

About 1840 it was a common sight between Dunbeath and Clyth Ness, on the coast of Caithness, for a fleet of between three and four hundred small brown-sailed boats to put to sea on a summer afternoon. A Presbyterian minister related that

'it is not unusual where there are boats having individuals of acknowledged piety, for the crew to engage in worship after shooting their nets. On these occasions a portion of a Psalm is sung, followed with prayer, and the effect is represented as truly solemn and heart-stirring as the melodious strains of Gaelic music, carried along the surface, several boats being sometimes engaged, spread throughout the whole fleet.' [21]

During the stirring 'Revival times' of 1860, the crews of herring drifters on the East Coast of Scotland often burst into a favourite

18 cf. A. Bosquet, *La Normandie romanesque* (Paris, 1845), p. 307.
19 E. Deseille, *Glossaire du patois des matelots boulonnais* (Paris, 1884).
20 cf. W. Jones, *Credulities, Past and Present* (1880), pp. 36–7.
21 *New Statistical Account of Scotland* (1845), Vol. XV, p. 88.

hymn or psalm as they were leaving the harbour for a night's fishing. When putting out to sea, the twenty-third psalm, *The Lord is my shepherd, I shall not want* was the favourite. When returning with a good catch, the hymn *O God of Bethel, by Whose Hand* was popular. A writer recalls that

'away out to sea could be heard the voices of the men as they were shooting their nets, singing *Jesu, Lover of my Soul* and *Rock of Ages, cleft for me,* and the custom was started at this time by many skippers of kneeling down in the cabin for prayer together before they would let down a net.' [22]

The belief that boats were often possessed by evil spirits was widespread until about a hundred years ago. Some curious rites were employed to exorcize them. On the coasts of Aberdeenshire and Banffshire there was the belief that certain persons, merely by looking at a boat, had the power to 'glower' fish away from it. It is related that

'when it was suspected that a boat had been forespoken, or the fish "glowrt oot o' the boat," she was put through the halyards. This was done by making a noose or "bicht" on the halyards large enough to allow the boat to pass through. The halyard with this noose was put over the prow of the boat, and pushed under the keel, and the boat sailed through the noose. The evil was taken off the boat.' [23]

This belief in the evil eye was not confined to Scottish fisher folk; it was just as common in Brittany. Greatly feared on the South West Coast of Brittany was a witch named La Kerzéas, who died in 1885, and who was alleged to have the *'drouk-avvis'* or evil eye. She used to prowl around the boats. One day she stopped beside a boat which had a good catch of conger-eels, and asked the skipper to give her one. He refused, so La Kerzéas 'glowered' on him and said: 'Instead of eels you will catch only dog-fish for the rest of the year.' [24]

But what made the possession of the evil eye so dangerous was that the malevolent glance could be directed mentally from a distance—there was no need for the witch to see the person or thing upon which she decided to work her spell. Thus in the case of a

[22] J. McGibbon, *The Fisherfolk of Buchan* (n.d.), p. 76.
[23] W. Gregor, op. cit., p. 199.
[24] H. le Carguet, in *Revue des Traditions populaires*, Vol. IV, p. 466.

boat, all she had to do was to get hold of something belonging to one of the crew, e.g. a piece of clothing, a lock of hair, or the parings of the nail.[25]

Then there were superstitions connected with theft. Fishermen in Finistère used to be certain that if any of the crew of a sardine boat had been associated with a theft, there would be bad luck until the stolen object had been returned to the owner.[26] On the other hand, when a boat on the North East Coast of Scotland was leaving home for another fishing station, for instance, during the herring season, some skippers borrowed an article of little value from a neighbour, but with no intention of returning it. The superstition was that 'the luck of the fishing went along with the article; those who were aware of the fact refused to lend.' [27]

There were German fishermen who were convinced that a stolen line brought luck to the robber, but took it away from the owner.[28] At Aberdeen there was the superstition that to lend some object to an adjacent boat took away all chance of good fishing to the owners.[29] Icelandic fishermen, if they wanted to injure an enemy, either rubbed sulphur on the hull of his boat or hid a small portion of this non-metallic element in a crack in her boards.

Burning nets or lines seems to have been an almost universal method of exorcizing fishing vessels. On the coast of Finistère it was the custom to burn damp straw to drive out the evil spirit by the smoke created. But he might be such a tiny devil that care was taken that the smoke penetrated into the smallest holes and cracks. Only when a boat had been thoroughly *'flambé'* would the sardines venture to swim into the nets. Burning straw was the traditional method of driving out the *Bosj* mentioned in Chapter Four.[30]

It is related that the fisher folk in an unspecified village on the coast of Yorkshire, which may have been Staithes, if a coble had had a spell of bad luck for a long time, used a grim method of exorcism. The wives of the crew met after dark, killed a pigeon, took out its heart, and pricked it with pins. Then they roasted the heart on a brazier. This ritual attracted the witch who was supposed to have cast a spell on the coble. When the women thought she had arrived they offered her presents.[31]

---

[25] cf. J. M. McPherson, *Primitive Beliefs in the North-East of Scotland*, p. 192.
[26] cf. G. de La Landelle, *Moeurs maritimes*.
[27] W. Gregor, op. cit., p. 200.
[28] B. Thorpe, *Northern Mythology* (1851–2), Vol. II, p. 111.
[29] W. Jones, *Credulities, Past and Present*, p. 116.
[30] H. le Carguet, in *Revue des Traditions populaires*, Vol. IV, p. 537.
[31] cf. P. Sébillot, op. cit., p. 218.

If the skipper of an open 'skaffie' or half-decked early type of 'baldie' or 'fifie' on the East Coast of Scotland about the middle of the last century suspected that she had been bewitched, the best thing he could do was consult a 'wise man' or a 'wise woman.' If he oiled his or her palm with silver, some amulet or charm would be handed over guaranteed to bring back luck with lines, nets or creels.[32]

When fishermen on the Ile-de-Sein found that no lobsters or cray-fish were tempted by the bait in the creels, they often made use of a traditional rite of exorcism. Another boat's net had to be stolen, and its corks burnt. Then a plate having been broken, the bits were put into the creels, to scrape the bark of the wooden hoops, the shavings of which were thrown into the fire.[33]

The malignant influence of witches, ghosties, kelpies, fairies, maukins and boggles of all sorts was suspected by many a fisher-man on the East Coast of Scotland during the first half of the last century if the hook of a line caught on a rock. Or he might attribute this to having met some 'ill-fitted' person immediately before putting to sea. Whoever hauled the line had to take to the bow of the boat a piece of seaweed or a shell-fish, spit on it, throw it into the water and spit again. This would avert the spell cast.[34]

Mermaids and mermen were both feared and loved.[35] Even as late as 1870 an old fisherman on the coast of Aberdeenshire swore that he had seen and conversed with a mermaid beneath the red granite cliffs near the Bullers o'Buchan, just north of Cruden Bay.[36] Fifty years before this it appears to have been a fairly general belief that the caves on this rocky coast were the homes of mermaids. A story was told that 'some old men remembered a mermaid pitching upon the bowsprit of a small vessel belonging to Peterhead, which was driven among the rocks near Slains Castle, and all hands perished save one man who bore the tidings to land.' [37] About the same time a mermaid with long yellow hair was said to haunt the shores of Cromarty Firth.[38]

[32] cf. *Folk-Lore Journal*, Vol. III, p. 181.
[33] cf. *Revue des Traditions populaires*, Vol. IV, p. 537.
[34] cf. *Folk-Lore Journal*, Vol. II, p. 181.
[35] The mermaid is part of British folk-lore. We can trace her from Corn-wall to John o'Groats; in Wales and in Ireland; we meet her in the folk-lore of the Hebrides, the Orkneys, the Shetlands, and the Isle of Man. In almost every instance the stories follow recognized patterns, and they embody the known beliefs about the mermaid' (Gwen Benwell and Arthur Waugh, *Sea Enchantress* (1961), p. 140).
[36] cf. Sir Hugh G. Reid, *Past and Present* (Edinburgh, 1870), p. 258.
[37] Peter Buchan, *Annals of Peterhead* (Peterhead, 1819), p. 41.
[38] cf. Hugh Miller, *Scenes and Legends* (Edinburgh, 1855), p. 286.

Here is part of a letter from George McKenzie, the schoolmaster of Rathven, Banffshire, printed in the *Aberdeen Chronicle*
of April 20th, 1814. He related that two fishermen at Portgordon,
a village about a mile west of Buckie, founded in 1797 by the fourth
Duke of Gordon, and for whose character and veracity he was able
to vouch, were returning from fishing in Spey Bay

> 'about three or four o'clock yesterday afternoon, when about
> a quarter of a mile from the shore, the sea being perfectly calm,
> they observed, at a small distance from their boat, with its back
> turned towards them, and half its body above the water, a
> creature of a tawny colour, appearing like a man sitting, with
> his body half bent. Surprised at this, they approached towards
> him, till they came within a few yards, when the noise made by
> the boat occasioned the creature to turn about, which gave the
> men a better opportunity of observing him. His countenance was
> swarthy, his hair short and curled, of a colour between a green
> and a grey: he had small eyes, a flat nose, his mouth was
> large, and his arms of an extraordinary length. Above the waist,
> he was shaped like a man, but as the water was clear, my in-
> formants could perceive that from the waist downwards, his
> body tapered considerably or, as they expressed it, like a large
> fish without scales but could not see the extremity.'

Then the man-fish dived, but rose again at some distance, and
to the increasing terror of the fishermen, they saw that he was
accompanied by what appeared to be a female of the same species,
since she had 'breasts.' Her hair reached a little below the shoulders.
This was enough: the men took to their oars and rowed hard until
they reached the safety of the little harbour among the rocks,
after which they got hold of the schoolmaster, and related their
experiences.[39]

Mermaids were also believed in by the more superstitious Breton
fishermen, as might be expected. Deep-sea sailors came home and
said that they had seen them on the ocean, as expressed in this
old song:

> *One Friday morn when we set sail,*
> *And our ship not far from land,*
> *We there did espy a fair pretty maid,*
> *With a comb and a glass in her hand.*

[39] cf. J. M. McPherson, op. cit., p. 73.

And the stormy winds did blow,
And we jolly sailor-boys were all up aloft
And the land-lubbers lying down below.[40]

Dr. Samuel Hibbert, writing in 1822, related that the Shetland fisher folk were convinced that beneath the depths of the ocean, an atmosphere existed adapted to the respiratory organs of certain beings resembling the human race, i.e. mermen and mermaids, the latter 'of surpassing beauty, of limited supernatural powers, and liable to the accidents of death.'

It was alleged that they had been seen off the Out Skerries, three islets five miles north east of Whalsay, where in those days there were extensive ling fisheries. Dr. Hibbert wrote that the Out Skerries were

'the particular retreat of the fair sons and daughters of the sea, where they are defended by a raging surf that continually beats around them, from the intrusive gaze and interference of mortals, here they release themselves from the skins within which they are enthralled, and assuming the most exquisite forms that ever were opposed to earthly eyes, inhale the upper atmosphere destined for the human race, and, by the moon's bright beams, enjoy their midnight revels.

These inhabitants of a submarine world were, in later periods of Christianity, regarded as fallen angels who were compelled to take refuge in the sea; they had, therefore, the name of Sea-Trows given to them, as belonging to the dominion of the Prince of Darkness.' [41]

On September 8, 1809, a Mr. William Munro, a schoolmaster at Thurso, in Caithness, had a letter published in *The Times*, where he set forth in detail the features of 'a figure resembling an unclothed human female, sitting upon a rock, extending into the sea, and apparently in the action of combing its hair, which flowed around its shoulders, and of a light brown colour.' He had been confronted by this mermaid about twelve years ago, when in charge of the school at Reay, about twelve miles west of Thurso, and while walking along the shore of Sandside Bay. He ended his long letter:

[40] The Mermaid, *Oxford Song Book*. Mermaid legends exist in almost all maritime folk-lore, and contact with these semi-human beings was generally believed to bring disaster in its train.

[41] *A Description of the Shetland Islands*. Shetland folk-lore contains many references to mermaids.

'It may be necessary to remark, that previous to the period I beheld this object, I had heard it frequently reported by several persons, and some of them persons whose veracity I have never disputed, that they had seen such a phenomenon as I have described, though then, like many others, I was not disposed to credit their testimony on this subject. I can say of a truth, that it was only by seeing the phenomenon, I was perfectly convinced of its existence.

'If the above narrative can in any degree be subservient towards establishing the existence of a phenomenon hitherto almost incredible to naturalists, or to remove the scepticism of others, who are ready to dispute everything which they cannot fully comprehend, you are welcome to it from,

Dear Sir,
Your most obliged, and most humble servant,
WILLIAM MUNRO.'

Caithness seems to have been the favourite resort of mermen and mermaids during the early years of the last century. There is the story of how a youth fell in love with a mermaid, and how she brought him gold, silver and jewels which she had taken from ships wrecked in the Pentland Firth. She enticed him to a cave near Duncansby Head, where he fell asleep. When he awoke he found himself enchained, unable to walk farther than a heap of diamonds and to the mouth of the cave.[42]

On October 29, 1811, John M'Isaac, a farmer living on the Mull of Kintyre, reported that he had met a mermaid at Campbeltown, and made a sworn statement before the Sheriff-substitute and the parish minister. Mr. M'Isaac must have had remarkable powers of observation and a retentive memory, for his description of this sea-creature runs to more than five hundred words. The Rev. Dr. George Robertson, the Rev. Norman MacLeod, and James Maxwell, Esq., Chamberlain of Mull, were 'satisfied that he was impressed with a perfect belief, that the appearance of the animal he has described was such as he has represented it to be.'

The following year, on August 11, 1812, a certain Mr. Toupin of Exmouth, affirmed that not only had he beheld a mermaid, but even heard her sing wild melodies, not unlike those of the Aeolian harp.[43] This apparition took place two years before the appearance of a merman and his mate off Portgordon in Banff-

---

[42] cf. Alex. Polson, *Our Highland Folk-Lore Heritage* (1926).
[43] cf. Alfred Gordon Bennett, 'The Mermaid Myth,' in *Focus on the Unknown* (1953).

shire, recorded already.[44] About 1830 some women cutting seaweed on the island of Benbecula in the Outer Hebrides told the story of how they had met a creature of female form playing happily off the shore. A few days later her dead body was picked up about two miles from where she had been first seen. It was recorded that 'the upper part of the creature was about the size of a well-fed child of three or four years of age, with an abnormally developed breast. The hair was long, dark and glossy, while the skin was white, soft and tender. The lower part of the body was like a salmon, but without scales.'[45]

In 1833 six Shetland fishermen, working off the Isle of Yell, reported that their lines had got entangled with a mermaid. They kept her on board their boat for three hours, and said that she was about three feet long. She 'offered no resistance nor attempted to bite,' but kept on moaning piteously. 'A few stiff bristles were on the top of the head, extending down to the shoulders, and these she could erect and depress at pleasure, something like a crest.' This mermaid had neither gills nor fins, and there were no scales on her body. The superstitious fishermen threw her overboard eventually, and related that she dived 'in a perpendicular direction.'[46]

A Mr. Edmondson, who heard the story from the skipper and crew, informed the Professor of Natural History at the University of Edinburgh that

'Not one of the six men dreamed of a doubt of its being a mermaid, and it could not be suggested that they were influenced by their fears, for the mermaid is not an object of terror to fishermen, it is rather a welcome guest, and danger is apprehended from its experiencing bad treatment. . . . The usual resources of scepticism that the seals and other sea-animals appearing under certain circumstances operating upon an excited imagination and so producing ocular illusion, cannot avail here. It is quite impossible that six Shetland fishermen could commit such a mistake.'

Indeed, it would have been unusual if these six fishermen had denied that they had caught a mermaid, because Shetland folklore contains many stories of creatures partly more than human, partly less so, which appear in the interchangeable shape of men

[44] See p. 122.
[45] cf. Alexander Carmichael, *Carmina Gadelica* (1900).
[46] cf. Dr. Robert Hamilton, *History of the Whales and Seals* (1839).

and seals. They are said to have often married ordinary mortals, so that even in the 1880s there were some alleged descendants of them who looked upon themselves as superior to ordinary human beings. Dr. Karl Blind wrote in 1881:

'In Shetland, and elsewhere in the North, the sometimes animal-shaped creatures of this myth, but who in reality are human in a higher sense, are called *Finns*. Their transfiguration into seals seems to be more a kind of deception they practise. For the males are described as most daring boatmen, with powerful sweep of the oar, who chase foreign vessels on the sea. At the same time they are held to be deeply versed in magic spells and in the healing art, as well as in soothsaying. By means of a "skin" which they possess, the men and women among them are able to change themselves into seals. But on shore, after having taken off their wrappage, they are, and behave like, real human beings. Any one who gets hold of their protecting garment has the Finn in his power. Only by means of the skin can they go back to the water. Many a Finn woman has got into the power of a Shetlander and borne children to him; but if a Finn woman succeeded in re-obtaining her sea-skin, or seal-skin, she escaped across the water. Among the older generation in the Northern isles persons are still sometimes heard of who boast of hailing from Finns; and they attribute to themselves a peculiar luckiness on account of that higher descent.' [47]

Brand's *Brief Description of Orkney, Zetland, etc.*, first published in 1701, states:

'There are frequently *Fin-men* seen here upon the Coasts, as one about a year ago on Stronsa, and another within these few months on Westra, a gentleman with many others in the Isle looking on him nigh to the shore, but when any endeavour to apprehend them they flee away most swiftly; which is very strange, that one man sitting in his little boat, should come some hundreds of leagues, from their own coasts, as they reckon Finland to be from Orkney. It may be thought wonderful how they live all that time, and are able to keep the sea so long. His boat is made of seal-skins, or some kind of leather; he also has a coat of leather upon him, and he sitteth in the middle of

---

[47] Article in *The Contemporary Review* (1881), quoted by David Mac-Ritchie, *The Testimony of Tradition* (1890), pp. 1–2.

his boat, with a little oar in his hand, fishing with his lines. And when in a storm he seeth the high surge of a wave approaching, he hath a way of sinking his boat, till the wave passes over, lest thereby he should be overturned. The Fishers here observe that these *Fin-men* or *Finland-men,* by their coming drive away the fishes from the coasts. One of these boats is kept as a rarity in the Physicians' Hall at Edinburgh.' [48]

The *Shipping Gazette* (June 4, 1857) felt it worth while to report that Scottish seamen somewhere off the coast of Britain had spotted a creature 'in the shape of a woman with full breast, dark complexion, and comely face.'

Mermaids were believed in by many a Cornish fisherman. Some went so far as to claim mermaid or merman ancestry, so Robert Hunt was told about 1846.[49] Nowhere around Britain were mermaids believed in so strongly as among the fisher folk of the Isle of Man, as was recorded by George Waldron in 1744.[50] He was told that few ships visited the island, and that this 'uninterruption and solitude of the sea, gave the mermen and mermaids (who are enemies to any company but those of their own species) frequent opportunities of visiting the shore.' More than one Manx fisherman swore 'by a thousand oaths and imprecations' that he had seen mermen and mermaids,

There was one crew which affirmed that they had found a mermaid in their herring drift-net. 'On examining their captive, by the largeness of her breasts and the beauty of her complexion, it was found to be female, nothing . . . could be more lovely, more exactly formed, in all parts above the waist resembling a complete young woman, but below that, all fish, with fins, and a huge spreading tail.' The fishermen took the mermaid ashore, but could not persuade her to eat or drink. At the end of three days, when 'she began to look very ill with fasting,' they opened the door of the house. She then glided on her tail to the beach, where she plunged into the sea. She swam away surrounded by a great number of her own species.

In the Channel Islands, mermaids were firmly believed in until living memory by old men and women. A Guernsey fisherman, then

---

[48] The so-called Hebridean 'Blue Men' were confined to a limited area in the Minch, and were a distinct species of mermen. They were said to haunt the Shiant Islands. Fishermen regarded them as weather controllers (see Donald A. Mackenzie, *Scottish Folk-Lore and Folk Life* (1935), Chapter IV, 'The Blue Men of the Minch').

[49] cf. *Popular Romances of the West of England.*

[50] *Description of the Isle of Man.*

in his ninetieth year, told Michael Marshall, who was collecting material for his book entitled *Herm—its Mysteries and its Charm*, published in 1958, that when he was a boy a mermaid market took place in Percée Passage, where the mermaids were tied to the pierced rock off Rosière Landing.

As recently as 1947 an eighty year old fisherman on the island of Muck, four miles north of Ardnamurchan Point, Invernessshire, related that he had seen a mermaid 'in the sea about twenty yards from the shore, sitting combing her hair on a floating herringbox, used to preserve live lobsters. Unfortunately, as soon as the mermaid looked round, she realized that she had been seen, and plunged into the sea. But no questioning could shake the old fisherman's firm conviction: he was adamant that he had seen a mermaid.' [51]

There were numerous safeguards against the power of witches and evil spirits when one was at sea. Small bags, sewn into the linings of jackets or inside jerseys, were much favoured. A Breton fisherman called such a bag his '*louzou*' or '*sachet magique*.' The story is told of an old sailor at Audierne, named Pobet-coz, who appeared to have extraordinary luck so long as he wore his *louzou*. One day it fell out because there was a hole in the lining of his jacket, and the *mousse* threw it overboard. From that moment Pobet had no better luck than any other fisherman, which convinced them of the virtues of the magic bag.[52]

It would be interesting to know if any seventeenth or eighteenth century fisherman on the south side of the Moray Firth ever had witches' bags, like the one Isobel Gowdie said she had made for the minister at Auldearn when he was sick in 1660. She confessed:

'We made a bag of the galls, flesh, and guts of toads, grains of barley, parings of the nails of fingers and toes, the liver of a hare and bits of clouts. We steeped this altogether all night among water, all minced into small pieces through other, and when we did put it among the water, Satan was with us.' [53]

Magic knots were much fancied by Moray Firth fishermen at one time, and they were obtainable from 'wise women.' She usually tied three knots on a bit of thread, after muttering an incanta-

---

[51] Gwen Benwell and Arthur Waugh, *Sea Enchantress* (1961), p. 261. This book is a mine of information on mermen and mermaids at all periods of history.

[52] H. Le Carguet, in *Revue des Traditions populaires*, Vol. IV, p. 467.

[53] R. Pitcairn, *Criminal Trials in Scotland* (Edinburgh, 1833), Vol. III, p. 609f.

tion. Then she told the man that if he wanted a light breeze he must untie the first knot; if a strong wind the second, but if he dared to touch the third knot, the result would be a gale.

There was a boat from Ardersier, where the fisher folk were very primitive and much given to superstition, which was forced to shelter on the west side of Tarbat Ness during a gale. Here they remained for several days, and eventually decided to consult the landlady of an alehouse, reputed to be a witch. She told them that the wind would change the following day. Before they left she gave them a length of wool with three knots, bidding them to treasure it. As the 'wise-woman' had prophesied, the wind veered to the north, and the crew hoisted their sail, and set their course in a sou'westerly direction. But they were curious to test the knots, and untied the first one, with the result that the wind increased in force. When they untied the second knot the wind freshened even more. In desperation they undid the third knot, whereupon the wind veered to the south, so the boat had to return to behind Tarbat Ness.

There was the belief at Portessie (otherwise known as Peterhythe or The Sloch), a village east of Buckie, that the first of the three magic knots ought to be untied as soon as a boat left the small natural haven among the rocks; the second when she was some distance from the shore. But the third knot must never be untied, for this would lead to a disaster of some sort. The story was told of a fisherman who had done this, with the result that a storm arose, and he was nearly drowned.[54]

In almost every country fishermen were terrified of the bright glowing light, caused by electrical discharge during storms, which often appears on the masts of vessels, and which is known as St. Elmo's Fire.[55] In Brittany there was the superstition that this bright light was the phantom of a near relative of one of the crew, who would die shortly. Elsewhere St. Elmo's Fire was believed to be the ghost of a drowned sailor.[56]

At one time fishermen at La Rochelle believed that to ensure good luck at sea there was nothing to beat gathering male ferns of certain species on the Vigil of St. John the Baptist, June 23rd, but this had to be done fasting and before sunrise. They plaited the

[54] cf. W. Gregor, in *Revue des Traditions populaires*, Vol. XII, p. 381.

[55] St. Elmo (or Erasmus), according to tradition, was a fourth century bishop at Formia in Italy, martyred under Diocletian. He is sometimes confused with St. Peter Gonzalez (or Telmo), a thirteenth century Dominican, who worked among fishermen on the coasts of Galicia.

[56] cf. E. and M. A. Radford, *Encyclopedia of Superstitions*, pp. 295–6; W. Gregor, in *Folk-Lore Journal*, Vol. IV, p. 7.

I

fern leaves into belts.[57] During the eighteenth century no fisherman on the Isle of Man ever went to sea without a few grains of
salt in a pocket. As late as 1879 there were salmon fishermen on
the Tweed who threw salt on their nets to drive away fairies.[58]

Elsewhere there was a belief in the magic qualities of tobacco.
The story is told of an old fisherman at Saint-Cast who always
spat over the sea the juice of the quid of plug tobacco he chewed,
being convinced that it attracted fish. Other fishermen believed that
tobacco smoke lured fish towards a boat, and often lit their pipes
expressly for this purpose.[59]

Another curious rite carried out by fishermen on the North
East Coast of Scotland to ward off evil spirits at sea, was to refer
by name to a man or woman alleged to be leading an immoral
life. Before shooting the lines one of the crew would say: 'We
will try the name of this or that woman who is a witch or living
in sin.' When a line had been paid out, another man would shout:
'Come up in the name of . . .' To complete the ceremonial, the
buoy at the top of the line had to be cut, while the name of
somebody supposed to be lucky was repeated.[60]

Some old fishermen on the coast of Normandy put their trust
in the mystic virtues of brandy, but it had to be kept in the same
bottle, and left until the bottle was impregnated with its smell.
Then a plank of the deck near the bows was lifted and the bottle
hidden beneath it. Great care had to be taken that there was no
sign of the plank having been removed. The superstition was that
once there was a bottle of very old brandy on board, the boat could
not fail to get big catches of fish.[61]

Just as on shore, there were many actions which could not be
done and remarks which could not be made when one was at sea.
It was strictly forbidden to play cards on any Dieppe fishing boat
at one time. On most Scottish fishing boats if a member of the
crew used the name of God when swearing, those who heard him
cried out 'cauld airn.' Every man then grasped the nearest bit of
iron, and held on to it for a few moments. This joint action, so
it was believed, averted the spell cast.[62] Suffolk fishermen shared
the same fear of swearing at sea; and so did those in Denmark.

Almost all seafarers in all ages have considered whistling to be
an ill-omened act, probably because it is a form of imitation

[57] Abbé Nogues, *Moeurs d'autrefois en Saintonge*, p. 148.
[58] cf. P. Sébillot, op. cit., p. 222.
[59] ibid., p. 223.
[60] W. Gregor, in *Folk-Lore Journal*, Vol. IV, p. 13.
[61] cf. P. Sébillot, op. cit., p. 224.
[62] E. E. Guthrie, in *Folk-Lore Journal*, Vol. VII, p. 45.

magic. To whistle is to imitate the voices of the wind and sea gods. It is related that Iceland fishermen extended this taboo to singing on their boats.[63]

In many countries there used to be a widespread superstition that fish would keep away from a boat, or some disaster occur, if certain words were used at sea. Shetland fishermen in olden times were afraid to refer to the sea itself. On no account could reference be made on a Scottish fishing vessel to a minister, kirk, pig, salmon, trout, hare, rabbit or dog.[64] As has been mentioned already, certain family names were regarded as equally ill-omened.[65] To nullify their evil, somebody had to spit. Spittle, like blood, was believed to be a centre of soul-power, and a potent agent of magic and protection.[66] At Buckie, Banffshire, as late as 1880, the fishermen were constantly 'spitting out bad names.'[67] Before hauling lines it was strictly forbidden to mention a horse, cow, dog, pig, hare, rabbit, rat, and certain other quadrupeds.[68] Shetland fishermen shared these particular superstitions. No member of the crew of a Dieppe fishing vessel ever dared to speak of cats when they were at sea.[69] Tailors and hares were greatly feared on the North Coast of Brittany. No fisherman would refer to them.

It is worth mentioning again that hares were regarded as unlucky in most parts of Europe, because of the widespread belief that witches turned themselves into hares.[70] Old fishermen at Audierne had an even greater fear of wolves. If anybody mentioned this animal at sea, it was enough to make a crew return to port at once. Not much more than half a century ago the *patron* of a boat belonging to this port on the South West Coast of Finistère used to throw the first fish caught into the sea, saying: 'There you are, Ki-coat (wolf), that belongs to you!'[71]

All four-footed animals were dreaded by Yorkshire fishermen, and were never spoken of by name when the boats were shooting or hauling lines or nets.[72] But pigs were the most ill-omened of all quadrupeds, not only on the coast of Yorkshire but also in most maritime countries.[73]

[63] F. S. Bassett, *Legends of the Sea*, p. 135.
[64] Rabbit Island, at the entrance to the Kyle of Tongue, Sutherland, was usually called 'Gentlemen's Island' by the Buckie fishermen to avoid using the unlucky word. They sometimes referred to pigs as 'grumphies.'
[65] See p. 100.
[66] cf. E. and M. A. Radford, *Encyclopedia of Superstitions*, pp. 318–20.
[67] cf. W. Gregor, op. cit., p. 200.
[68] W. Gregor, in *Revue des Traditions populaires*, Vol. VI, p. 662.
[69] A. Bosquet, *La Normandie romanesque*, p. 308.
[70] cf. Radford, op. cit., pp. 181–2. See also p. 104.
[71] H. Le Carguet, in *Revue des Traditions populaires*, Vol. VI, p. 536.
[72] cf. P. Sébillot, op. cit., p. 233.
[73] See pp. 102–3.

Rats were both feared and venerated, because it was believed that they could convey warnings of death or misfortune. In some Scottish fisher communities both rats and mice led to a lot of 'spitting out.' For superstitious reasons many fishermen would not eat pork, or even duck and goose.[74] Yet taken all round, salmon always remained the most dangerous word, and it involved endless circumlocution, e.g. 'the red fish,' 'the beastie-fish,' 'the fish with scales,' 'the foolish beast,' or simply 'the beastie.' If any member of a crew was so foolish as to breathe the word salmon, one of his shipmates ejaculated instantly: 'Deel cut oot yer ill tongue.' [75]

At Pitulie, and elsewhere on the coast of Buchan, there was an almost equal fear of mentioning a green-crab, especially when shooting or hauling lines. It was difficult to avoid speaking of it because it was used for bait. The only thing to do was to refer to a 'snifftie fit.' [76] This is far from being a complete list of all the words and objects which coulid not be spoken of at sea in fishing vessels, for every country had its own taboos.

It was fairly common with Breton fishermen before they shot their lines, nets or creels, to invoke the sea-birds or fishes, using certain traditional verses. At Saint-Cast, for instance, the sea was invoked as follows:

> *Mer, cesse tes tribulations,*
> *Amène-nous du poisson*
> *Pour nourrir les garçons.*

To drive away sea-gulls and other birds, this incantation was employed:

> *Oiseaux, restez chez vous à dormi',*
> *Car si vous venez ici,*
> *Vous allez avoir un coup d'fusi'.*

On the Newfoundland Banks fishermen put their trust in a longer prayer to drive away skate from the lines intended for cod.

> *Rais, quitte nos hameçons,*
> *Va chez les autres qui t'en remercieront;*
> *Va t'en donc sur les bancs du Léjon!*

---

[74] W. Gregor, in *Revue des Traditions populaires*, Vol. IV, p. 660.
[75] W. Gregor, in *Folk-Lore Journal*, Vol. III, p. 182. Elsewhere salmon were known as 'charlies' or 'gentlemen.' The present generation of Scottish fishermen has more or less forgotten the fear their ancestors had of this word.
[76] Gregor, op. cit., p. 148.

Maudites raies de Miquelon.
Les pècheurs l'y prendront:
Au lieu de t'couper l'nez comme nous l'faissons,
Ils te mettront dans leurs bateaux
Et ne te rejetteront point à l'eau.

Innumerable verses of this sort were used to attract fish or drive away diabolical influences.[77]

So many were the vernacular exorcisms, mostly in rhymed verse, recited by Breton fishermen in olden times, that an interesting collection of them could be published. When the crews of boats shooting lines for mackerel off Cap Fréhel noticed young sardines, one of them would say:

Maudite haguette, voleuse d'affare [*bait*]
Tu ressembles au minard:
Sauve-toi d'ici et ne reviens pas,
Ou bien tu y périras.

Jolie poule de mer,
Viens sous notre bateau,
Chasser cette haguette,
Qui fait peur aux maquereaux;
Tu vas te régaler de manceau
Que nous jetterons pour te récompenser dans l'eau.

Crabs were regarded as sea-devils, and greatly feared. It was safer always to crush a crab, and say:

Des pêcheurs jamais vous ne serez aimés,
Mais toujours haïs vous serez,
Puisque vous les maudissez.[78]

Similar rhymed exorcisms and blessings were employed for many other species of fish all round the coasts of Brittany. They were also used by Sussex fishermen. When a Brighton 'hogboat' shot their nets about a hundred years ago, the men bared their heads and chanted: 'There they goes then. God Almighty send us a blessing it is to be hoped.'

Richard Jefferies (1848–87), whose books deal mainly with natural history, described the Brighton fishermen about a hundred years ago as still 'quite separate and belonging to another race.'

[77] cf. P. Sébillot, *Le Folk-Lore des Pêcheurs*, pp. 236–43.
[78] cf. *Revue des Traditions populaires*, Vol. III, p. 596.

When shooting drift-nets for herring they observed the following
ritual: as each barrel (which was attached to every two nets out
of the 120 usually shot) was cast overboard, the crew would cry:

> *Watch, barrel, watch! Mackerel for to catch,*
> *White may they be, like a blossom of a tree.*
> *God send thousands, one, two, and three,*
> *Some by their heads, some by their tails,*
> *God sends thousands, and never fails.*

When the last net was overboard the skipper said: 'Seas all!'
Then the foremast was lowered and the sturdy little hog-boat laid
to the wind. If the skipper were to say, 'Last net,' he would expect
never to see his nets again.[79]

A more elaborate ritual was sometimes observed by Sussex
fishermen when shooting nets, in which all the crew took part. The
skipper began by saying:

> *Now, men, hats off!*
> *God Almighty send us a blessing through Jesus Christ. Amen.*

Then each of the eight men forming the crew continued with his
own formula:

FIRST MAN: Watch barrel! Watch
           Mackerel for catch.
SECOND MAN: White may they be, like a blossom.
THIRD MAN: Some by head.
FOURTH MAN: Some by tail.
FIFTH MAN: May God send us mackerel. May he never fail.
SIXTH MAN: Some by nose.
SEVENTH MAN: Some by the fin.
EIGHTH MAN: May God send as many as we can lift.[80]

The Brighton fishermen of the old breed, who wore copper-hued
'frocks' and trousers as thick as boards, had a superstition that
what they called the 'Moon line,' i.e. the moon's reflection on the
surface of the water, brought bad luck if it passed over lines.[81]

On the Yorkshire coast, fishermen's children when they saw
the moon used to pray:

---

[79] cf. R. Thurston Hopkins, *Small Sailing Craft* (1931), pp. 121–2.
[80] F. E. Sawyer, *Supplemental Notes on fisheries* (Brighton, 1884), p. 4.
[81] ibid., p. 5.

I see the moon and the moon sees me,
God bless the sailors on the sea.[82]

The Bretons did not only invoke the sea, winds and fishes to bring them good luck; they also made use of many traditional prayers to God and the saints. Around the Bay of Saint-Malo there was this verse:

Sainte Marie, mère des flots,
Faites la grâce que nous prenions quelques maquereaux.
Des petits et des gros.

The oyster fishermen at Saint-Cast used to recite:

Va au bon Dieu,
Prends garde de t'perd'e,
Et reviens t'en pleine.[83]

The pious Catholic crews on the Biscayan coast of Spain said after each fish caught, *Ave Maria purissima.*[84]

The sardine fishermen on the coast of Morbihan performed an even more intricate ritual before shooting their nets than that used by the Brighton herring fishermen. The *patron* took out a bottle of holy water kept in the stern of the boat and handed it to a fisherman in the bow, who uncorked it. Each member of the crew in turn put his finger into the bottle as it was passed round, ending with the *patron*. Then each man made the sign of the cross, and the nets were shot. When this was done, the *patron* sprinkled a few drops of holy water over the rest of the gear, and also over the boat, in two directions. After this a prayer wes said, often improvised.[85]

Yet there were quite as many fishermen who regarded human spittle as having much greater magical power than holy water. Spitting not only averted evil, as has been related, but it was believed to have all sorts of beneficial results. The crews of boats on the estuary of the Gironde below Bordeaux not only spat on each worm that baited a line, but also on the water as often as possible, convinced that this would attract fish. German fishermen are said to have indulged in a ritual spitting of lobster-pots; and cer-

[82] E. and M. A. Radford, *Encyclopedia of Superstitions*, p. 238.
[83] P. Sébillot, op. cit., pp. 246–7.
[84] ibid., p. 246.
[85] G. de La Landelle, *Moeurs maritimes*, p. 138.

tain English fishermen used to spit on the anchors of their boats.[86]
The *Girondais* had another curious superstition; they rubbed
between their legs the first shad caught.[87]

Special attention was usually paid to any first fish caught. At
Saint-Cast everything depended on who brought it aboard; if it
was a man with a 'lucky hand' the prospects were good; if, on the
contrary, it was somebody with a 'bad hand,' then the worst could
be expected.[88] On the North Coast of Spain, the member of a crew
who brought the first tunny-fish on deck was given two litres of
cider, paid for by the others.[89] On some drifters from ports on the
North East Coast of Scotland there used to be great curiosity to
find out if the first herring that was shaken out of the nets was
male or female; if the former, then the season would be bad; if
the latter, it would be prosperous. Altogether there were so many
species of fish regarded as unlucky if caught first, that it would
take up too much space to mention them in detail. Some had to be
thrown back into the sea; others killed at once.

When fishing for conger eels, the skipper of a boat from one of
the ports on the coast of Asturias used to recite the following verse:

> *Hola! hola! hola!*
> *Anima sola*
> *Que el señor le perdone.*

The man who caught the first eel said: *'Bendito y alabado sea el
santisimo Sacramento!'* The rest of the crew replied: *'Par siempre
sea benedito alabado.'* [90]

[86] C. de Mensignac, *La Salive et le Crachat* (Bordeaux, 1892), p. 77.
[87] F. Daleau, *Traditions et superstitions de la Gironde* (Bordeaux, 1889),
p. 47.
[88] cf. P. Sébillot, op. cit., p. 254.
[89] Braulio Vigon, *Folk-Lore de la Mar*, p. 19.
[90] B. Vigon, op. cit., p. 16.

Chapter Nine

RETURN TO PORT—FISHWIVES AND THE SALE OF FISH

IN some ports it used to be the custom for the fisher folk to celebrate the return of the boats after a long spell at sea with great rejoicings. At Cancale, for instance, the crews of the *bisquines* often danced on the decks as the fleet sailed into the harbour at high tide if they had done well on the famous oyster beds. This fishing, known as the *caravane*, started during the second fortnight of April.[1]

The Le Pollet fishermen at Dieppe, and in certain other ports on the coasts of Upper Normandy, used to chant a *Te Deum* as their luggers sailed into harbour at the end of the herring season.[2] In olden times in ports around Finistère it was the custom for the boat which went out to investigate if the sardines had appeared off the coast, to have its mast adorned with flowers should a shoal of sardines have been found. The first basket of these little silver fish landed was known as *'le bouquet,'* and it was carried through the streets of the village at the head of a procession.[3] Shetland fisher folk had the superstition that if a cat were seen running along the shore before the return of the boats, it was an omen of a good fishing.[4]

When the two-masted schooners with a single square-tops'l on the fore, each carrying a crew of eight or nine men, returned to Paimpol after fishing for cod off Iceland for the whole of the summer; or when the larger barquentines came back to other ports in Brittany and Normandy from the Newfoundland Banks, there was a great welcome given them by the women who had been left behind. Nearly always there were babies for fathers to gaze at for the first time. For as Pierre Loti wrote in his novel *Pêcheur d'Islande*: 'This race of fishermen which Iceland devours can do with many children.' He continued:

'Then a month or two later, when all the fleet has returned, save those which had been lost at sea, the *Pardon des Islandais* takes place on 8th December, Feast of the Immaculate Con-

[1] E. Herpin, *La Côte d'Emeraude* (Rennes, 1894), p. 80.
[2] A. Bosquet, *La Normandie romanesque*, p. 307.
[3] G. de La Landelle, *Moeurs maritimes*, p. 138.
[4] cf. K. Blind, in *The Gentleman's Magazine* (1882), p. 253.

137

ception of Our Lady, Star of the Sea. Under the grey skies of winter, more often than not in an atmosphere of drizzling rain, the crews of the *"goëlettes"* gave vent to the pent-up emotions of their six or seven months' enforced repression at sea in an outburst of savage enjoyment. But it was a brutal, sullen mirth, with nothing of the natural vivacity and lightheartedness of southern races; rather a challenge to destiny and fate; a wish to forget the hardships and privations of those long weeks of grinding, monotonous toil day after day that they had gone through off Iceland, with its storms of blinding rain and chill winds. They craved nothing better than to feel the grateful warmth of alcohol in their bodies, the rousing of all their dormant physical passions and animal lust, so that they could forget for a time the overhanging menace of another year's fishing before them.' [5]

Similar orgies took place in many a pub at Hull and Grimsby when the sailing smacks returned from long spells of beam-trawling or shooting great-lines on the North Sea; living in conditions which were quite as primitive as those in the French schooners and barquentines. But in the English ports there was no statuette of the Blessed Virgin standing on a bracket in a corner of the bar, where she looked down on the fishermen, drinking and smoking their little black clay pipes with the bowl turned down, in an atmosphere of intense heat, clouds of tobacco smoke, with the smell of brandy, rum, wine and cider mingled with that of damp clothes and sweating humanity; a terrific din of voices, shouting, singing and swearing. For the most part the English fishermen stuck to beer when they were ashore for a few days, but fights and brawls were just as frequent as in the French ports. So too were the brothels patronised by the fisher lads, judging from reports published in the 1880s.

In most fisher communities on the East Coast of Scotland where there was no harbour it used to be the custom for the women to take the fish, lines and other gear off the boats when they got back to the shore, but on no account would they have ventured aboard them, for this would have brought bad luck.[6] It was also usual for the fish to be divided among the crew. Each man marked his share by some object, e.g. a knife or a stone, which was placed on the heap of fish.[7] For superstitious reasons, just as much as from

---

[5] op. cit., Part I, Chapter II.
[6] W. Gregor, in *Revue des Traditions populaires*, Vol. IV, p. 663.
[7] W. Gregor, *Counting Rhymes of Children* (Edinburgh, 1891), p. 8.

motives of generosity, it was advisable to give away plenty of
herring to anybody who asked for a 'fry.' Then there were also
some curious superstitions connected with the sale of the first basket
or box of fish, for instance, it was wiser not to deal with anybody
who had large thumbs.

Some English fishwives used to spit on the first coin received
when selling fish. The Boulogne women were more pious and said:
'J'vas faire au nom du Père pour que ça me porte bonheur.' [8]

Most fishwives in Scotland took care to look out for purchasers
with 'lucken feet,' and to avoid 'ill-fitted' persons. They were
scared if anybody pointed to them while they were selling fish.
In the Buchan District, as elsewhere, 'they left home by a very early
hour in companies of tens and scores. As they proceeded, one went
off here, and another there, each to supply her own customers. The
bulk of them went to the country villages, at which they commonly arrived at an early hour, in time to supply newly cured
fish for breakfast. They often beguiled their long way—ten, twelve,
fifteen, and twenty miles—with song. In the villages the fish was
sold for money, but in the country districts they were exchanged
for meal, potatoes, sids (seeds), turnips, and even if money were
given, something in the way of barter had to be added. The creel
was often carried home heavier than it was carried out.

'In the outward journey, if the weather was stormy, companies
of women took possession of the houses by the wayside, if the
doors had been left unbarred. After the male inmates left for the
barn to thresh, it was usual for one of the females of the family
to get up, and secure the doors against their entrance. The railway
has modified all this.' [9]

It was much the same in almost all parts of France. At Cibourne,
a small fishing village near Saint-Jean-de-Luz on the borders of
Spain, women (known as 'Cascarottes') used to think nothing of
walking twenty miles to Bayonne, laden with heavy baskets of
sardines and anchovies, singing traditional songs.[10]

Fisher life in the old days was basically matriarchal because
the wife ruled the home. A century ago James Bertram wrote:

'Of necessity a fisherman's wife is extremely masculine in
character. Her occupation makes her so, because she requires a
strength of body which no other female attains, and of which

[8] E. Deseille, *Glossaire du patois des matelots boulonnais.*
[9] W. Gregor, *Notes on the Folk-Lore of the North-East of Scotland*
(1881), p. 202.
[10] cf. P. Sébillot, op. cit., p. 277.

the majority of men cannot boast. The long distances she has frequently to travel in all weathers with her burden, weighing many stones, makes it essential for her to possess a sturdy frame, and be capable of great physical endurance. Accordingly, most of the fishwives who carry on the sale of their husbands' fish possess a strength with which no prudent man would venture to come into conflict. Then the nature of their calling makes them bold in manners, and in speech rough and ready. Having to encounter daily all sorts of people, and drive hard bargains, their wits, though not refined, are sharpened to a keen edge, and they are more than a match for any "chaff" directed towards them either by purchaser or passer-by. So long, however, as they are civilly and properly treated, they are civil and fair-spoken in return, and can, when occasion serve, both flatter and please in a manner by no means offensive. Altogether, the Scottish fishwife is an honest, out-spoken, good-hearted creature, rough as the occupation she follows, but generally good-natured and what the Scotch call "canty." She does not even want feeling, though, it may be, her vocation gives her little opportunity to show it. But who is so often called upon to endure the strongest emotions of fear, suspense and sorrow, as the fisherman's wife? Every time the wind blows and the sea rises, when the boats of her husband or kinsfolk are "out," she knows no peace till they are in safety; and not seldom has she been doomed to stand on the shore and look at the white foaming sea in which the little boat, containing all she held dear, was battling with the billows, with the problem of its destruction or salvation all unsolved.' [11]

At Fisherrow, the fishwives used to make the journey to and from Edinburgh, carrying a heavy load of fish in the creel on their backs. If the boats happened to be late, it was not unusual for the women to perform the six or seven miles journey by relays, three carrying one basket, shifting it to the other every quarter of a mile or so. Sometimes they covered the distance in three-quarters of an hour to an hour. There is a story that on one occasion three Fisherrow women did the twenty-seven miles journey from Dunbar to Edinburgh on foot, each with 200 lbs. of fish on her back, in five hours. As might be expected their amusements were masculine. They played golf long before it was adopted by ladies of the 'upper classes.' On Shrove Tuesday there used to be a football match at Musselburgh between the married and unmarried Fisherrow women. They were renowned for their rude eloquence, but it was

[11] op. cit., pp. 323-4.

recorded by the parish minister that 'their licentiousness in speech
is not accompanied by licentiousness in morals.'

When George IV visited Edinburgh he declared that the Newhaven fishwives were the handsomest women he had ever seen.
Like their rivals at Fisherrow they usually wore a long blue duffle
jacket, with wide sleeves, a blue petticoat tucked up so as to form
a pocket, and in order to show off their ample under petticoats of
bright-coloured woollen stripe, reaching to the calf of the leg.
The upper petticoats were made of different coloured drugget. As
the women carried their load of fish on their backs in creels, sup-
ported by a broad leather belt resting forwards on the forehead,
a thick napkin was their usual headdress, although a muslin cap,
or mutch, with a very broad frill, edged with lace, and turned back on
the head, was seen peeping from under the napkin. A variety of
kerchiefs or small shawls similar to that on the head encircled the
neck and bosom, which, with thick black worsted stockings, and
a pair of black leather shoes, completed the costume.

It was recorded of the typical Newhaven fishwife about a hundred
years ago:

> 'She is always supposed to ask double or triple what she
> will take; and, on occasions of bargaining, she is sure, in
> allusion to the hazardous nature of the gudeman's occupation,
> to tell her customers that "the fish are no fish the day, they're
> just men's lives." The style of higgling adopted when dealing
> with the fisher folk, if attempted in other kinds of commerce,
> gives rise to the well-known Scottish reproach of "D'ye tak' me
> for a fishwife?" ' [12]

Towards the close of the eighteenth century great quantities of
fish were brought by women to Aberdeen from villages to the south
and north, even as far as Newburgh, fifteen miles distant. It is
recorded that

> 'these poor drudges will thus travel fifteen miles before breakfast,
> with a heavy load upon their backs; and such is the force of
> habit, that they would think it a punishment to be obliged to
> return home without a load in their baskets, equal in weight to a
> third of their outward-bound cargo. If so they have neither goods
> nor provisions to carry home, they generally take in ballast of
> stones, and thus they trudge homeward with four shillings in
> their pockets, the produce of the fish; which if purchased from
> fishermen, produces a clear profit of one shilling.' [13]

[12] Bertram, op. cit., p. 426.
[13] John Knox, *View of the British Empire, more especially Scotland*
(1784), p. 503.

James Bertram wrote in 1865 that the fishermen at Aberdeen
did nothing but catch the fish, and said:

> 'Just now there are many fishermen who will not go to sea
> as long as they imagine their wives have got a penny left from
> the last hawking excursion. The women enslave the men to their
> will, and keep them enchained under petticoat government. Did
> the women remain at home in their domestic sphere, looking
> after the children and their husbands' comforts, the men would
> pluck up spirit and exert themselves to make money in order to
> keep their families at home comfortable and respectable. There
> is no necessity for the females labouring at out-of-door
> work . . .' [14]

It was much the same sort of situation in many other fisher communities on the East Coast of Scotland a hundred years ago. At
Whitehills, Banffshire, for instance, in addition to attending to
their domestic duties, the women baited their husbands' lines,
prepared fish for sale, and hawked it round the country-side. We
are told that the fishwife 'is allowed an influence which in any
other condition of life would appear little consistent with either
feminine propriety or domestic order. She usually claims the entire
proceeds of the white fishing, which lasts ten months of the year,
as her exclusive prerogative.' [15]

In 1793 the women at Buckie, Banffshire, led very strenuous lives.
They dragged up the boats on the rocky foreshore and launched
them again. Rather than allow their husbands and sons to get
their feet wet before going to sea, they took them up in their arms
and carried them aboard their boats, doing the same when they
returned from the fishing. When the boat was afloat, the women
had to hand on board the ballast and lines to the crew. It was not
unusual on a winter's day for them to be wet to the height of the
waist.[16]

The women at Avoch on the Black Isle, Ross-shire, also used
to carry the fishermen on their backs to keep their feet dry. Aided
by their children, they gathered bait, prepared the lines and culti-
vated hemp. Brought up on a diet consisting mainly of oatmeal,
potatoes and fish, the Avoch folk were a hardy race; the women
as strong as the men. They thought nothing of hawking around
the country a hundred pound weight of fish in their creels. It is

[14] op. cit., p. 450.
[15] *New Statistical Account of Scotland* (1845), Vol. XIII, p. 220.
[16] cf. George Hutchison, *Days of Yore* (Buckie, 1887), p. 21.

recorded that 'except for a few days about Christmas, or on the occasion of a fisher's wedding, there are none but little children idle in the whole Seatown of Avoch.' [17]

What has been related about the fishwives in Scotland applies almost equally well to those in England and France during the last century. They ruled their husbands in just the same way, and kept a firm hold of money. On the Ile-de-Sein the women not only did all the work ashore, but even owned the land. Sometimes a husband was ignorant of the exact locality of the field on which his wife and daughters worked.

Except in a few places where trawling was the method of catching white fish, lines were used in the smaller communities on the coasts of almost every country in Northern Europe until early in the present century. This meant that most of the women were kept busy baiting lines for seven or more hours daily when the boats were at sea. Having got her husband and sons off to their day's work about dawn, the wife, perhaps accompanied by one or two of her daughters, put on her warmest clothing and went down to the shore, if it was low tide, to gather mussels. Each line fisherman usually owned a 'scarp' of mussels, and kept them alive in pools among the rocks. Crouching on probably slippery seaweed-covered rocks, the women plunged their hands into the water, and took away from one to two thousand mussels, carrying them home in pails.

Then the wife sat down on a low chair in her kitchen, or outside in fine weather. She took several shells in her left hand, and opened them with a sharp pointed knife, dropping the bait into a bowl on her lap. More likely than not, she had to stop after an hour or so to give the younger children their breakfast, and see them off to school. For the rest of the morning she went on shelling mussels until she had enough bait.

Next came the much more delicate work of putting the bait on to the lines, which had been left to dry overnight from the previous day's fishing. The lines were neatly coiled in baskets or trays, the shape of which differed according to the district or country. They were known in Britain as 'scowls,' 'swills,' 'skeps,' or 'rib-boards.' Each line was about 300 fathoms (1,800 feet) long, with about 500 hooks attached to it at intervals. Every day two lines had to be baited. The woman put the basket or tray on her left side, sat down on a chair, with a large wooden scoop or trough propped up at her right side in a convenient position. She drew the lines over her knees, undid every hook, and fixed on the soft bait. If the mussels were small, two or three were needed for every hook.

[17] *The Statistical Account of Scotland* (1793), Vol. XV, pp. 625ff.

The baited hooks were arranged in close rows at the shallow end of the trough, and the lines coiled at its deeper end. As the lines had to be placed so that they could be shot smoothly over the gunwale of the boat, the greatest care had to be taken lest one hook became entangled with another.

When the men-folk returned from their day's fishing—the inshore boats seldom fished at night—each usually carried a basket of wet lines under an arm. Sometimes their weight was relieved by a cord across the shoulders. Sooner or later came the job of cleaning every hook. This was not always done in quite the same way, but one method was first to hang the two dripping lines on a pole where they were disentangled. The hooks were attached to the lines, first by a whipcord-like 'snood,' made of twine, then a length of plaited horse-hair, or several thicknesses of twine.[18] This formed a strong pliable 'spreader' or 'sprawl' which kept the snood from fouling the main line. It was fixed to the hook with strong linen thread. In the old days every self-respecting fisherman made the whippings and joins himself. In some districts white horse-hair was believed to bring better luck than any other colour.

Very often a fisherman's wife had to continue her baiting during the afternoon, while her husband started to arrange his lines for the following day's baiting. Seated on a chair, with a line laid carefully on the seat of another chair, he got to work. Beside him was an empty basket. He passed the whole line through his hands, over his knees, into the basket. Every inch of line had to be examined carefully lest rocks had rubbed or weakened it. A rough loop was made in any weak part, so that it could be cut out and spliced. Each snood had to be scrutinized. The job might have to be carried on after the family had finished their evening meal. In winter time, when the only light was from candles or a small lamp, it was a great strain on the eyes.

Not only had the average inshore fisherman's wife to spend the greater part of her day baiting lines, she also had to keep the house clean, cook, and do other domestic jobs, such as darning, ironing, knitting and baking. It was almost a week's work getting all the thick woollen underwear worn by the men and boys washed and dried in winter. There were no washing-machines or spin-driers. Few fishing villages had water laid on in the houses. It usually had to be carried in from a well or pump, and heated on the open fire. Not every house had a shed with special provision for washing clothes.

[18] It had various names, e.g. on the East Coasts of England and Scotland, a 'tippet'; in Devon and Cornwall, a 'gangeing.'

It is not surprising that fishermen had to take good care to choose wives who were strong in body and able to assist them with their daily work, as was explained in a previous chapter. A bride had to be selected in much the same manner as a new boat, a net, or any other kind of fishing gear. She was regarded not only as a breeder of children, but also as a human 'tool.' In addition, as has been related already, one of her jobs was to walk many miles around the country-side, selling fish.

K

Chapter Ten

DISEASES AND DEATH

BESIDES the healing charms prescribed by witch-doctors, male and female, mentioned already, fisher folk in olden times resorted to other ways of curing diseases which were not connected directly with black or white magic, but which for the most part were superstitious in character.

On the North East Coast of Scotland there were various cures for epilepsy. After the first fit the clothes had to be stripped off, and burned on the spot where the patient fell. It was recommended that he or she should put on a shirt in which somebody had died, and wear it without it first being washed. Another cure was to draw blood from the left arm after the first attack. If somebody present had never before seen an epileptic fit, then he or she might be able to prevent another attack by pricking the sufferer's little finger.[1] Fisher folk on the Côtes-du-Nord in Brittany believed that epilepsy could be cured if the patient was laid on a certain kind of seaweed found on the shells of crabs, and known as *'gui marin.'* But it had to be gathered on Easter Day at three o'clock in the morning by a man having a clear conscience. At Erquy, a fishing village about half way between Cap Fréhel and Saint-Brieuc, it was said that this miraculous weed could sometimes be found on the head of a gurnet and that occasionally the sea washed it up on the beach.[2]

The fisher-mother of a rickety bairn in the Buchan District of Aberdeenshire could resort to either of the following cures. She took the child to a blacksmith, who filled a tub with water then plunged pieces of hot iron into it. After this he took the child from the mother, dipped it in the water, and gave it a little of the water to drink. The second ritual was more elaborate. The bairn had to be taken before sunrise to a smithy and where three men of the same name worked. One of them bathed the patient in the water-trough. Having been dried, the child was laid on the anvil, and all the tools in the shop passed over the body one by one. Then a second ritual bath followed. No fee could be asked by the black-smiths, and all three had to officiate.[3]

[1] W. Gregor, *Notes on the Folk-Lore of the North-East of Scotland,* pp. 41–2.
[2] P. Sébillot, in *Archivio per lo studio delle tradizioni popolari,* p. 518; and *Folk-Lore des Pêcheurs,* p. 61.
[3] W. Gregor, op. cit., p. 45.

Lumbago, rheumatism and sprains were common complaints. There was a superstition that persons born with their feet first could cure all of them, either by rubbing the affected part of the body, or tramping on it. 'Skate-bree,' i.e. the water in which this fish had been boiled, was also regarded as a cure for rheumatism by fisher folk on the North East Coast of Scotland.[4]

Few people can have escaped toothache at one time or another. and there was a common belief that it was caused by a worm at the root of the tooth. For this reason the pain was often simply called 'the worm.' One superstitious cure was to carry on one's body the following verse, written on a slip of paper:

> *Peter sat on a stone weeping.*
> *Christ came past and said, 'What aileth thee, Peter?'*
> *'O, my Lord, my tooth doeth ache,'*
> *Christ said, 'Rise, Peter, thy tooth shall ache no more.'*

In some places this charm could be bought, rolled in a neat packet and sealed.[5]

If toothache became unendurable, the best thing to do was to go to the nearest kirkyard when a grave was being dug, look for a skull with teeth in the jaws, lift a stone from it with the teeth, and the pain would vanish.[6] A mother dreaded to see that a baby had cut its first tooth in the upper gum, for then it would be short-lived. There was the verse:

> *The bairn it cuts its teeth abeen,*
> *Ill nivver see its mairidge sheen.*[7]

Any pain in the eyes could be cured in the following manner, according to the peasantry in the North East of Scotland, but it was not easy. Somebody had to catch a frog, and lick its eye with his tongue. The person who had done this had merely to lick the eye of the sufferer with his tongue, and the pain would go.[8]

Should there be an epidemic of whooping-cough in any fishing district, some very superstitious methods were used to cure the victims. One was to make them eat a plateful of 'pushlocks,' i.e. the boiled excrements of sheep. Another involved taking the patient

---

[4] ibid., p. 46. See p. 24.
[5] cf. W. Henderson, *Notes on the Folk-Lore of the Northern Counties of England and the Borders*, p. 172.
[6] ibid., p. 145.
[7] ibid., p. 20.
[8] W. Gregor, op. cit., p. 46.

to the house of a married woman whose maiden name was the
same as that of her husband, and let her give the bairn some 'pushlocks' to eat. The milk of an ass was sometimes given as a remedy
for whooping-cough; so was a draught of water from the hollow
of a detached boulder.[9]

Warts could be cured in several ways. One went to a point where
four roads met, lifted a stone, rubbed the warts with the dust
below the stone, and repeated this charm:

> *A'm ane, the wart's twa,*
> *The first ane it comes by*
> *Taks the warts awa.*

Or one could rub the warts with a snail; or rub it with a piece of
meat, bury the meat, and as it decayed, so the wart disappeared.[10]

If these methods proved ineffective, then the wart could be
rubbed on a man who was the adulterous father of a child, but
this had to be done without his knowledge. There are other
strange methods by which it was believed that warts could be
cured.[11]

Ringworm, which must have been fairly common in the un-
sanitary conditions in which most fisher families lived during the
first half of the last century, had its superstitious cure in rubbing
the diseased spot with silver. The ritual and ceremonial were as
follows:

> 'Put a new shilling three times round "the crook," spit a
> "fastin spittle" on it, and with it rub the affected part. Some,
> in addition, dropped the shilling through the patient's shirt before
> rubbing with it.'

Or a decoction of spurge, known as 'little gueedie' or 'mair's
milk,' was used as a lotion.[12]

One of the cures for what was called the 'sleepy fever' involved
a complicated ritual:

> 'The patient's stocking was taken and laid flat; a worsted
> thread was placed along both sides of it over the toe. The stock-
> ing was then carefully rolled up from the toe to the top, so that

---

[9] ibid., p. 46.
[10] cf. Henderson, op. cit., p. 139.
[11] cf. W. Gregor, op. cit., p. 19.
[12] ibid., p. 47.

the two ends were left hanging loose on different sides of it. This stocking was put three times round each member of the body contrary to the course of the sun, beginning with the head. The left of two members was taken first. When the stocking was passed round an affected member the thread changed its position from outside to inside; but when the member was sound the thread kept its position. The process was gone through three times, and in perfect silence. The thread was afterwards burned.' [13]

There was another alleged cure for 'sleepy fever,' which involved taking three stones from a burn, and performing a complicated rite with fire and water, which was repeated for three nights in succession.

What was known as 'casting the heart' was one of the most extraordinary cures used by the poorer folk in the Buchan District of Aberdeenshire in olden times. It took two forms, and this was the more elaborate one:

'The operator, who was generally an old woman renowned for her medical skill, set the sieve on the patient's head, and on the sieve she placed the "three-girded cog," for no other dish was of any virtue. The comb was placed on the bottom of the cog, and the water was poured through one of the loops of the scissors into the cog. Lead was melted and dropped through the same loop. After the heart-shaped piece was found, the patient took three draughts of the water in the cog, and washed the hands and face with the remainder, which was thrown over a place where the dead and the living cross, that is, a public road. The patient might either bury the piece of lead or keep it most scrupulously under lock and key. During the process the operator kept repeating the words, "Ghen onything be oot o's place, may the Almichty in's mercies fesst back." ' [14]

Drinking three draughts of water into which iron or silver had been cast was also a cure for the evil-eye or 'forespeaking.' [15]

All around the coast of Brittany the fisher folk had traditional cures for various diseases similar in character to those found on the North East Coast of Scotland. They put great faith in magic potions made from certain kinds of seaweed, guaranteed to cure almost any sickness.[16] In Lower Brittany there was a belief that

[13] ibid., p. 44.
[14] ibid., p. 43.
[15] See pp. 103, 119.
[16] P. Sébillot, op. cit., p. 61.

invalids suffered more pain on a rising tide, and that death usually took place then. Around Saint-Malo, the superstition went in the other direction; a fisherman never died except when the tide was on the ebb.[17]

Death omens were believed in by fisher folk in almost all countries of northern Europe. One of the most common was an apparition of the still living or dead person. In Brittany there was a widespread superstition that if a man died at sea his mother or wife would be told of it in some paranormal manner. A bird would tap on the window pane, or a drop of blood would appear on her hand or on the floor, or she would hear water dropping near her head.[18]

Very often a woman refused to believe in the death of her husband, son, or other near male relative at sea unless she had received an *avènement* or warning.

At Saint-Cast there was a conviction that if a man died on shore when his boat was at sea, one of the crew would be given an omen at the moment he expired. It could take several forms, for instance, a star of unusual brightness, or a strange light about the height of a man on the water.[19] Scandinavian fishermen had a superstition that before a man died the oars of his boat were turned round during the night by invisible hands, and that this would be discovered the following morning.[20]

The womenfolk at Paimpol, when they had received no news of the fishermen working off Iceland, and feared for their safety, used to make a pilgrimage to Saint-Loup-le-Petit, between Plouëzec and Plouha, where they lit candles before the image of the saint in the chapel. If the flame burned brightly they took it as an omen that all was well for the man for whom they prayed. If the flame flickered or went out, they had no doubt that he was dead.[21]

Almost everywhere around the coast of Brittany the *Ankou* was dreaded, because he was the personification of death itself. The last man to die in any parish before the end of the year became the *Ankou* during the following year, acting as the Watcher of the graveyard. People who saw him said he was a tall, lean man with long white hair. More often than not his face was over-shadowed by a wide-brimmed felt hat. In some places he took the form of a skeleton shrouded in a white sheet, his head spinning round on his

[17] See p. 152.
[18] P. Sébillot, op. cit., p. 62.
[19] ibid., p. 64.
[20] cf. O. Nicolaissen, *Sagen og eventyr pra Nortland*, p. 8.
[21] Anatole Le Braz, *La Légende de la Mort chez les Bretons* (Paris, 1895), Vol. I, p. 8.

vertebral column like a top, so that he could embrace in one glance the whole region he was visiting. Elsewhere he dragged a cart, all black, but occasionally it was driven by a headless coachman, and harnessed to a team of scraggy horses. There were stories that the *Ankou* had also been seen with two macabre companions; the one held the bridles of the horses, and the other ran on ahead, opening gates, and knocking on the doors of houses where death would soon take place. If somebody within was already near his end, he died while the cart stood outside. There were curious beliefs about the origin of the *Ankou*. Some said that he was a spirit specially created by God to summon the dying; others that he was Adam's eldest son, 'condemned by his father's sin to lead men to the grave, or the soul of a man who blasphemously denied God while he lived, and was henceforth compelled to serve death for evermore.' [22] No matter: the Breton fisher folk as well as the farmers had no doubt that it was Death himself who prowled around their shores or who drove along the lanes at night.[23]

Fisher folk on the North East Coast of Scotland had their own death omens. The most common took the form of three knocks heard at regular intervals of one or two minutes' duration. The sound might be heard in any part of the house—on a table, on a door, or on the ceiling of the box-bed. People said that it was dull and heavy and had something eerie about it.[24] Then there was the so-called 'dead-drap,' which resembled that of a steady dripping of water, with a leaden and hollow sound. These death omens were usually heard at night, and by one person only, unless somebody else in the room took hold of the one who first heard the sounds.

Another warning of an immediate death was a light called the 'dead-can'le' or 'corpse-light.' It either took the form of a ball of fire, or a flame pale-blue or yellow in colour, unlike the light given by an ordinary candle or oil-lamp. A murmur of many human voices around the door of the house was yet another death omen on the North East Coast of Scotland. So too was the crowing of a cock before midnight. A dog howling at night was also a portent of death. So too were three drops of blood falling from the nose. This meant that some near relative would soon die. Much more alarming was the apparition of the person doomed to die within

---

[22] E. and M. A. Radford, *Encyclopedia of Superstitions*, p. 102.

[23] Churchyard watchers, similar to the Breton *Ankou*, were believed in also in parts of England, Wales, Ireland, and the Scottish Highlands.

[24] cf. W. Gregor, *An Echo of the Olden Time from the North of Scotland* (Edinburgh and Glasgow, 1874), p. 132.

a short time. It could be seen during the day as well as after dark; and it is not surprising that whoever beheld the ghost often fainted, because it was wrapped in a winding sheet. There was the superstition that the higher the sheet reached up towards the head, the nearer was death.[25]

On some parts of the coast of Finistère there was a superstition that if the father, brother or husband of the invalid were at sea, he or she would not die until the rising tide, and the return of the relatives.[26]

The belief that death took place at low water, common on the North Coast of Brittany, also existed in East Anglia until well on in the last century. Charles Dickens recalled it in *David Copperfield*.

' "He's going out with the tide," said Mr. Peggotty to me, behind his hand.

'My eyes were dim, and so were Mr. Peggotty's; but I repeated in a whisper, "With the tide?"

' "People can't die, along the coast," said Mr. Peggotty, "except when the tide's prettty nigh out. They can't be born, unless it's pretty nigh in—not properly born, till flood. He's a going out with the tide. It's ebb at half-arter three, slack water half an hour. If he lives till it turns, he'll hold his own till past the flood, and go out with the next tide."

'We remained there, watching him, a long time—hours.

' " He's coming to himself," said Peggotty. Mr. Peggotty touched me, and whispered with much awe and reverence: "They are both a going out fast."

' "Barkis, my dear! " said Peggotty.

' "C. P. Barkis," he cried faintly. "No better woman anywhere! "

' "Look! Here's Master Davey! " said Peggotty. For he now opened his eyes.

'I was on the point of asking him if he knew me, when he tried to stretch out his arm, and said to me, distinctly, with a pleasant smile: "Barkis is willin'."

'And it being low water, he went out with the tide.'[27]

On the Moray Firth coast, and elsewhere in Scotland, curious

[25] ibid., pp. 134–5.
[26] P. Sébillot, *Légendes, Croyances et Superstitions de la Mer* (Paris, 1886–7), Vol. I, p. 132.
[27] op. cit., Chapter XXX.

ways of finding out whether an illness would end in death were practised. The Kirk Session Records of the fishing village of Cullen (1649) relate that:

> 'it was remembered that Marjorie Palmer, having a sick child, and wishing to know if the child would live or die, digged two or three graves. One she called the dead grave and another the living grave, and asked a woman (who did not know that Marjorie had done this) to go with the child and put him in one of the graves, for she believed that if the child was put in the living grave he would live, and if in the dead grave he would die. Therefore the said Marjorie, being accused, confessed that she did it out of ignorance by the information of a woman whom she knew not. Marjorie was debarred from the Sacrament by order of the Presbytery.' [28]

Another ritual was to dig two holes in the ground, between which the sick person was laid, without being told which was meant to be the grave of the living or of the dead. If he turned his face to the latter he would die, and if in the opposite direction he would live.[29]

The ceremony known as *La Proella* appears to be still common on the Isle of Ushant (Ouessant); the most remote of all the numerous islands off the coast of Brittany, ten miles from the mainland of Finistère, surrounded on all sides by granite cliffs, and often shrouded in dense fogs. The majority of the male inhabitants serve in the *marine-marchande* or in the *marine-de-guerre*, the rest being fishermen. All the older women are dressed in black, with their hair flowing down to their waists.

As soon as the news of a seaman's death has been received on Ushant by the civil authorities, his oldest male relative is informed. It is his duty to visit houses occupied by kinsfolk of the deceased to announce the death to them; usually with the formula: 'This is to state that this evening there will be the ceremony of *La Proella*.'

Not until after dark does he dare approach the house of the widow. Then he knocks three times gently on a window. Having entered the door he says: 'To-night, my poor child, the *Proella* will take place here.' The female relatives, who have already heard the news, hurry in and mingle their cries and groans with those of the dead sailor's family. This ritual wailing is called *mener le deuil*. Meanwhile a room is cleared out; a white cloth laid on a

[28] W. Gregor, op. cit., p. 205.
[29] ibid., p. 204.

table, upon which are placed two napkins folded in the shape of a cross. In their centre rests a wax cross made of bits of the candles blessed and distributed on Candlemas Day, February 2nd. This cross is meant to represent the body of the dead man. A small dish, filled with holy water, and a bunch of leaves, are placed close by, also two lighted candles. Very soon mourners arrive from other parts of the island. One of them, known as a *prieuse,* recites all the usual prayers for the departed, and sometimes preaches a sermon, known as a *prézac.* Next morning the clergy and acolytes appear as if for an ordinary funeral. They remove the 'corpse,' i.e. the little wax cross, and carry it to the church; followed by a procession of bare-headed men and women with black shawls drawn close over their faces. The cross is laid on a catafalque in front of the altar. After the Requiem Mass the priest puts the cross in an urn-shaped box or casket fixed to the wall of the chancel. Here it remains, either until the next All Souls' Day, or until some other solemn occasion, such as a parochial mission. Then all the crosses in the urn are removed to a special tomb in the midst of the cemetery, which serves as a common 'grave' for the wax symbols of the bodies of men who have died at sea far away from their island home surrounded by the Atlantic. A similar ceremony takes place on the Ile-de-Sein when one of the men dies at sea or too far away for his body to be brought back.[30]

At one time there was the superstition at Whitby that whenever a fisherman was buried, a spectral coach appeared on the day after his funeral. It was drawn by six black horses and accompanied by two outriders in black bearing lighted torches. The black-robed coachman hid his face as he drove at a furious pace to the church-yard on the hill above the harbour. A crowd of ghostly mourners were alleged to walk round the grave until the dead man rose from his coffin and followed them into St. Mary's Church near the Abbey ruins. Here they remained in the box-pews and galleries until after midnight, when they came out, jumped into the coach, and were driven at a mad rate down the narrow winding streets until they vanished mysteriously.[31]

Fisher folk in Brittany used to be sure that when a man died at sea, gulls and curlews flew around his house and beat their wings against the windows. On the Ile-de-Sein stories were told of the *Crierien*—the rattling of the bones of sailors whose souls wanted a Christian burial. There were some fisher communities where it

---

[30] cf. P. Sébillot, *Le Folk-Lore des Pêcheurs,* pp. 65–6; and Ch. le Goffic, *Gens de Mer,* p. 255; P. F. Anson, *Fishermen and Fishing Ways* (1932), pp. 43–4.
[31] cf. H. S. Gee, *The Romance of the Yorkshire Coast.*

was believed that a storm would continue until the corpses of seamen who had died in sin had been thrown up on some shore. The
souls of those who had been drowned at sea, or whose bodies had
been buried in unconsecrated ground, were believed to be doomed
to wander eternally along the shore. Their piteous cries could be
heard after dark—*'Iou! Iou!'* When fisher folk in Finistère thought
they heard strange sounds above the howling of the wind on a wild
night, they said: *'E-man Iannic-ann-od o Iouall!'* ('There is Iannic-
ann-od crying out! '). The restless souls of drowned seafarers were
harmless enough unless one imitated their cries. This was dangerous, for they might break the neck of the imitator. On the Isle
of Ushant people were sorry for poor *Iannic-ann-od*, and said he
wanted a fire to warm himself when he sighed or moaned beneath
the door, or whistled through the chinks of a window. Both Cornish
and East Anglian fishermen used to say that drowned seafarers
could be heard wailing in storms.

Maritime folk-lore contains frequent references to the belief that
the spirits of the dead are shipped to a land in the West, where
the sun goes down.[32] Gervase of Tilbury (*c*. 1150–*c*. 1220), a
medieval English writer, refers to the 'soul-ship' in his *Otia
imperialia*, which he composed for the instruction and entertainment of Emperor Otto IV, when he was living at Arles. This is how
the story is given by the Rev. S. Baring-Gould in *A Book of Folk-
Lore:*

'On a certain feast-day in Great Britain, when the congregations came pouring out of churches, they saw to their surprise
an anchor let down from above the clouds, attached to a rope.
The anchor caught in a tombstone; and though those above
shook the cable repeatedly, they could not disengage it. Then the
people heard voices above the clouds discussing apparently the
propriety of sending some one down to release the flukes of
the anchor, and shortly after they saw a sailor swarming down
the cable. Before he could release the anchor he was laid hold
of; he gasped and collapsed, as though drowning in the heavy
air about the earth. After waiting about an hour, those in the
aerial vessel cut the rope, and it fell down. The anchor was
hammered out into the hinges and straps of the church door,
where, according to Gervase, they were to be seen in his day.
Unfortunately he does not tell us the name of the place where
they are to be seen.' [33]

[32] 'Hy Brazil' is the name given to this land in Irish legends.
[33] op. cit., pp. 153–4.

Breton fisher folk believed that the granite cliffs on the coast of Finistère and the quiet waters of the Golfe-du-Morbihan were specially favoured by soul-ships.

But the Bay of Souls, near the Point-du-Raz—the real 'Land's End' of Brittany—was the most used spot for gathering together the spirits of the departed, awaiting transport to the Isles of the Blessed.

Cornish fishermen in olden times also believed in phantom ships, sailing over land and sea, after death occurred. Sometimes they arrived along with squalls and gales. There is the story of a wrecker, whose 'last moments were terrible, a tempest taking place in his room, where the plashing of water was heard.' Another Cornish folk-lore tale relates how the soul of a notorious white witch was carried off in a black barque 'with all her sails set, and not a breath of wind stirring.' [34] Then there was once a pirate who lived at Priest's cove.

'At his death a cloud came up, with a square-rigged ship in it, and the words, "The hour is come, but not the man," were heard. As the ship sailed over the house, the dying man's room was filled with the noise of waves and breakers, and the house shook as the soul of the wrecker passed away, borne in the cloud ship.' [35]

On parts of the coast of Normandy fisher folk used to be convinced that the soul ship arrived on All Souls' Day.

'The watchman of the wharf sees a vessel come within hail at midnight, and hastens to cast it a line; but at the same moment the boat disappears, and frightful cries are heard that make the hearer shudder, for they are recognized as the voices of sailors shipwrecked that year.' [36]

The belief that the souls of the departed are transported across water is found in Celtic, Greek, Scandinavian, and even Hindu folk-lore. The stories in various forms are found in almost every maritime country.[37]

[34] ibid., p. 155.
[35] ibid., p. 155.
[36] ibid., p. 164.
[37] Captain Marryat's novel *The Phantom Ship* (1839) and Richard Wagner's opera *Der Fliegende Holländer* (1843) are founded on the legend

The departed were always very much alive to the Breton fisher folk. Those at Port-Blanc, a village facing the Ile Saint-Gildas and the more distant Sept-Iles, believed that the ghosts of drowned men were sometimes seen landing on the shore in search of fresh water; walking up the beach in a silent procession. Anatole le Braz, the great authority on Breton folk-lore, who lived at Port-Blanc, was told that when the fishermen of Trévou-Tréguinec, a nearby village, embarked at night they beheld the hands of male corpses clinging to the sides of their boats. Sometimes there were female bodies, but they kept farther off, with their long hair floating on the surface of the water. Very often the oars got entangled in the dripping hair.

Le Braz also relates how a certain fisherman at Port-Blanc once told him that he had been walking along the shore at night in search of flotsam and jetsam. His foot knocked against something which emitted a hollow sound and rolled away towards the edge of the water. He looked for the object and was disappointed to find that it was merely a human skull, so he chucked it away. Suddenly a low wailing noise was heard out at sea. The terrified fisherman saw what he said were thousands of arms rising out of the water. At the same time, so he maintained, invisible hands tried to drag him away from the net he was carrying. It occurred to him that he ought to have shown more respect to the skull, so having found it, he replaced it on the exact spot where his foot had knocked against it. He confided to Le Braz that he was sure that if the skull had fallen into the water he would have been doomed, saying: 'All those arms that waved at me so desperately would have dragged me into the sea.' [38] Granted that the fisherman may have been drunk, the point of the story is that his brain turned instinctively to the para-normal, that he was certain he had met ghosts.

After a shipwreck in the Bay of Douarnenez the fisher folk believed that the sea carried the bodies into the Grotte-de-l'Autel, near Morgat, on the north side of the Bay, where their souls reposed for eight days before entering purgatory. It was dangerous to disturb the drowned bodies during this interlude of repose by venturing into the cave.

As has been related already, there was an almost universal belief in fisher communities until recent times that it was unlucky

---

of a phantom ship which, in consequence of a murder committed on board, is supposed to haunt the sea in a perpetual effort to make Table Bay, and seen in stormy weather off the Cape of Good Hope.
[38] *La Légende de la Mort chez les Bretons* (Paris, 1893), Vol. I, p. 398.

to try to save anybody from drowning.[39] This was to deprive the
spirits of the ocean of the sacrifices they demanded. On the North
East Coast of Scotland, as in some other countries, it was regarded
as 'ill-luckit' even to touch the corpse of a drowned man or to
bring it ashore.

The fear of rescuing drowning men from a wreck is mentioned
by Sir Walter Scott in his novel *The Pirate*, published in 1822.[40]
Cornish fisher folk used to affirm that the sea could always be heard
calling for one of its victims. The Revd. S. Baring-Gould tells the
following story.

'A fisherman or a pilot walking on the sands at Porth-Towan,
when all was still save the monotonous fall of the light waves
upon the sand, distinctly heard a voice from the sea exclaiming,
"The hour is come, but not the man." This was repeated three
times, when a black figure, like that of a man, appeared on the
top of the hill. It paused for a moment, then rushed impetuously
down the steep incline, over the sands, and was lost in the sea.' [41]

When the Revd. Walter Gregor published his *Folk-Lore of the
North-East of Scotland* in 1881, he wrote: 'Everything is changing,
and changing faster than ever. The scream of the railway engine
is scaring away the witch, and the fairy, and the ghost.' [42] Nevertheless he was in time to collect some interesting facts about
traditional superstitions connected with death which had survived
in the country districts and along the coasts of the counties of
Aberdeen and Banff: some of which he had also found in William
Henderson's *Notes on the Folk-Lore of the Northern Counties of
England and the Borders,* first published in 1879.

Usually the dying person was removed from the box-bed and
laid on the floor. When anybody appeared to be struggling hard
for breath, or as it was said, 'hid a sair faicht,' some object was
broken above the head. There was a superstition that this action
helped the heart to stop beating. The moment that death occurred
all the doors and windows that could be opened were thrown open.

[39] See pp. 97, 101.
[40] He collected Orcadian and Shetland folk-lore stories on a voyage with
the Scottish Lighthouse Commissioners.
[41] *A Book of Folk-Lore*, pp. 114–15. R. Hunt, in *Popular Romances of
the West of England* (two series, 1865 and 1881) states that this story in
different forms is told all round the Cornish coast.
[42] How surprised he would have been if told that eighty years later,
railway engines would have vanished from the Buchan District of Aberdeenshire, and that almost all the lines would be closed.

The idea was that this allowed the departing spirit full egress, and prevented evil spirits stopping it.[43]

After this all sorts of things had to be done. The chairs in the house were sprinkled with water, also the clothes of the deceased. If there was a clock, it was stopped. Pictures and mirrors were covered with white cloths. In some fishing villages all the butter and onions were thrown away; and all the milk was poured out on the ground.[44] To prevent death entering into meal, cheese, flesh, or whisky, a piece of iron, for example a nail or a knitting-wire, was stuck into them. Hens and cats had to be shut up until the body was buried. There was a superstition that if either of them leaped over a corpse, the first person to meet the hen or cat would eventually become blind. In one fishing village on the North East Coast of Aberdeenshire, not a single spadeful of earth was moved during the whole time that the corpse was unburied.[45]

Mr. Gregor relates that:

'When the death took place a messenger was despatched for a wright, who hasted to the house of death with his "strykin beuird." The body was washed, and after being clothed in a home-made linen shirt and stockings, it was "strykit" on the board brought by the wright, and covered with a home-made linen sheet. Many a bride laid up in store her bridal-dress, to be made into her winding-sheet, and her bridal linen and bridal stockings, as well as her husband's, to be put on when life's journey was ended.'

Each fisher village had its own variant in funeral ritual and cere-monial. At Ferryden, on the coast of Angus, the beadle of the parish kirk of Craig, early in the last century, having 'houked,' i.e. dug, the grave, with the earth still clinging to his boots, and clad in a sleeved waistcoat and corduroy trousers, could be seen in the streets, with their heaps of mussel-shells and fish-offal, on his way to the house where a death had occurred. He had the 'mortcloth' carefully folded under one arm, while over the other shoulder were two 'spokes' on which the coffin would be carried to the kirkyard, nearly a mile from the village. The beadle placed them on either side of the door, and laid the cloth on a chair set in the entrance. Sometimes the 'spokes' were put against the doorway many hours

---

[43] Gregor, op. cit., p. 206; Henderson, op. cit., pp. 53–6.
[44] Gregor, op. cit., pp. 206–7; Henderson, op. cit., p. 56.
[45] ibid., p. 207.

before they were required, to remind passers-by that a funeral was about to take place.

There were no undertakers or ready-made coffins in those days, so it might take time before the joiner or 'wright' arrived with the coffin, and the corpse laid within it. The mortcloth was spread over it with much ceremony and care.[46] The usual custom was to place a saucer or plate containing a little salt on the breast to keep the evil spirits away.[47]

A survival of Catholic custom was found in one or two candles kept burning beside the dead body. There existed the superstition that, if one of the candles overturned and set fire to the grave-clothes, it proved that the deceased had led an evil life, or even sold his soul to Satan.[48]

A messenger, usually the beadle of the parish kirk, invited, or 'warnt,' people to the funeral, but before this there was the so-called 'lyke-wake,' after the corpse had been laid in the coffin, which was attended by more intimate friends and relations. Until the funeral an unbroken watch or 'waukan' was kept beside the coffin, above all during the night.

'A few of the neighbours met every evening, and performed the kind office of watchers. One of them at least had to be awake, lest the evil spirits might come, and put a mark on the body. The time was ordinarily spent in reading the Scriptures, sometimes by one, and sometimes by another of the watchers. . . . All conversation was carried on in a suppressed voice.

'Sometimes the "waukan" was not so solemn. Practical jokes have been played upon the timid. Some stout-hearted one placed himself within the "bun-bed" beside which the dead lay, and, when those on whom the trick was to be played had entered the house, and taken a seat, he began to move, at first gently, and then more freely, imitating as far as possible the voice of the dead, to the utter terror of such as were not in the secret.

'There was a plentiful supply of new pipes and tobacco, procured specially for the occasion, and hence the irreverent sometimes spoke of the "lyke" as the "tobacco-nicht." Whisky was also freely given, and in many cases tea, or bread and cheese with ale were served about midnight.' [49]

---

[46] cf. D. H. Edwards, *Among the Fisher Folks of Usan and Ferryden* (Brechin, 1921), p. 229.

[47] Gregor, op. cit., p. 207; Henderson, op. cit., p. 56. Blessed salt has been used for liturgical purposes from very early times.

[48] Gregor, op. cit., p. 208.

[49] ibid., p. 209.

The traditional 'lyke-wake' was often denounced in the Kirk Sessions Records during the seventeenth and eighteenth centuries. They appear to have been bacchanalian orgies in some places, with what are described as 'lascivious exercises, sports, bawdy songs, fiddling, dancing and gaming.' John Ramsay wrote of them after visiting the North East of Scotland:

'Nothing went on in the house of mourning but dancing and other amusements. Even the ties of nature and affinity seem to have been suspended, for a widow who had just lost her husband, her and her infant's only support, was constrained by the fashion to suppress her sorrow, and to join in the expression of joy and merriment. The nearest relation of the deceased, together with the stranger of most distinction, commonly began the dance. . . . There are strong traces of this custom not only among Eastern Highlanders but even among the bordering Lowlanders not long ago.' [50]

The Scottish peasantry when taking part in a typical lyke-wake had much in common with African savages beating tom-toms to keep away malignant devils from a corpse. Then there was also the fear that the spirits might recognize the persons at a 'waukan,' so there was dressing-up; the women changing clothes with the men, and vice versa. For the same reason the room was often turned upside down, and all the chairs overturned.

Sometimes the chairs were never used again, lest the ghost of the departed, if he returned to earth, should recognize his house by the furniture.

To enable the deceased to pay his fare to whatever future state he would enter, it was customary to put a silver coin in the coffin. Then it was also the rule for every watcher to lay his or her hand on the head or breast of the corpse, to show that there was no quarrel with the dead.[51]

Among the Catholic fisher folk in France the nocturnal watchings were more religious in character. A ritual meal took place after midnight, where a place was laid for the deceased. The belief was that by partaking invisibly of the food and drink he or she would be given strength to endure the period of purgation before obtaining perfect bliss. It was not enough to pray for the soul of

[50] *Scotland and Scotsmen in the Eighteenth Century* (1888), p. 328; see also Thomas Pennant, *A Tour of Scotland* (1769), p. 49.

[51] cf. J. M. McPherson, *Primitive Beliefs in the North-East of Scotland*, p. 125.

Fisher Folk-Lore

the dead person whose corpse was present. Many a *De Profundis* was recited for every deceased member of the family whose names could be recalled. In Presbyterian Scotland, however, to pray for the dead was regarded as a popish superstition.

Moreover the Protestant Reformers in Scotland forbade any sort of religious service at the graveside because of their strong aversion to prayers for the dead. Ministers were allowed to give 'words of counsel' in the kirk before and after the burial, but they were forbidden to offer prayer, lest by chance they suggested that the soul of the departed was in purgatory and could be assisted by prayer. Even to-day it is the custom to hold a brief service in the house before the coffin is removed by the undertakers, at which only members of the deceased's family are present. It is also the custom in Scotland for no women to assist at the graveside rites. The female relatives remain in the house to prepare a meal for the male mourners on their return from the cemetery.

Until about the middle of the last century, when the day of the funeral arrived, a room was specially arranged. On the table were new clay pipes and a good supply of cut plug tobacco; likewise plates laden with bread and cheese. Below the table stood bottles of ale and whisky. Each male mourner as he entered, if he were a smoker, took a pipe, filled and lit it. When all the guests had assembled the parish minister or an elder, seated in an arm-chair, offered prayer in an atmosphere of tobacco smoke instead of incense. Sometimes it was a member of the family who took the place of the minister. Then came the ceremonial drinking of toddy. Mr. Gregor recalls that

'There have been those who were famous for their joviality in their lifetime giving strict orders on their death-bed regarding the quantity of whisky to be used at their funeral obsequies. When the toddy was made and tested, all glasses were filled and handed round. They were emptied to the memory of the departed. Bread and cheese followed. The glasses were filled again and drained to the toast, "Consolation to the friends of the deceased." Then came more bread and cheese, and a glass or two more of toddy. Such as preferred "a drap o' the raw geer," or ale, to the toddy received it. When all had eaten or drunken in a manner befitting the station and means of the dead, prayer was again offered; not, however, always. It was then announced, "Gehn ony o' ye wis t'see the corp, ye'll noo hae an opportunity." The company thereupon one by one went into the apartment of death, uncovered his head, and gently and reverently laid his hand upon the breast or brow of the dead, frequently making a remark on the appearance of the body, as "He's unco like himsel," "She's a bonnie corp," or "He's said altert"; or on the character of the departed, as "She'll be a sehr misst unmman," or "He's wiz a gueede freen t' ony ane." It was believed that unless the body was touched the image of it haunted the fancy. If the body was soft and flabby when the coffin-lid was closed, it was a sure indication that another corpse would at no distant period of time be carried from the same dwelling.' [52]

Usually the coffin was carried out of the house and laid on two chairs. The wooden 'spokes,' mentioned already, were then placed under it. Covered with the mort-cloth, it was borne to the graveyard, the bearers relieving each other at intervals. As soon as the coffin had been lifted off the chairs, they were overturned, and left to lie, either until after the burial or until sunset. They had to be washed before being used again. Very often there was more drinking of whisky at the grave side, and bread and cheese were handed round. Then the more intimate friends and relatives returned to the house for a festive meal.

In some places in the North East of Scotland a circuit was made sunways by the mourners round some spot near the grave; the idea being that this would deceive the spirit of the departed if he returned to earth. At Garmouth, Morayshire, they took the corpse round a building known as the house of the Holy Ghost which stood near the kirkyard. It is recorded that 'they could not be restrained from this superstition till the walls were quite razed of late.' [53]

In one village, apparently in the Buchan District of Aberdeenshire, so Mr. Gregor relates, it was the custom the night after the funeral for bread and water to be placed in the room where the body had laid. For it was believed that the dead returned that night, being hungry and thirsty. Until refreshed, the spirit could not find peace in the unseen world. [54]

In spite of Calvinist theology repudiating the belief in any sort of intermediate state, and teaching that men and women go straight to heaven or hell according to their predestination from all eternity, the peasantry in the North East of Scotland throughout the seventeenth and eighteenth centuries were generally convinced that the

---

[52] op. cit., pp. 210, 211; also Henderson, op. cit., p. 57.
[53] L. Shaw, *History of the Province of Moray* (Edinburgh, 1775), Vol. III, p. 385.
[54] op. cit., p. 213.

spirits of the departed return to earth and hold converse with friends and relations. The Kirk Session Records often refer to search being made for persons alleged to be conversing with familiar spirits.[55]

Graveyards were feared, as were all articles associated with death—coffins, mort-cloths, and above all human bones. Tombs were believed to be haunted by the ghosts of those who had committed some crime, and could not find rest because of their guilty consciences. Both the fisher and country-folk believed that these lost souls

'appeared nightly in hope of coming in contact with some living person bold enough to meet them, and to whom they could make known their sin, and to whom they could tell what to do for them to remove the load, and thus allow them to rest at peace in their graves. Such graveyards were avoided after nightfall, and made many a benighted traveller take a roundabout way home if it lay before him in his journey.' [56]

Persons who in their lifetime had sold their souls to the Devil were said to visit kirkyards at midnight. Stories were told of men who wanted to acquire the power of 'arresting' man or beast; and who prowled around graves after dark, where they dug up a coffin, took one of the lid screws, and repeated the Lord's Prayer backwards. Earth from graves was believed to have magic qualities.

Although none of the Kirk Session Records appear to contain specific reference to fisher folk conversing with familiar spirits, some of the places mentioned in them are near enough to the sea to make it probable that they shared the same superstitions as the country folk. For instance, the records of the Synod of Moray about the middle of the seventeenth century mention that two men confessed to having seen a little boy who appeared to them, and then suddenly vanished, and that they never beheld this apparition again.[57] At Dyce, only five miles from the Aberdeenshire coast, a certain Thomas Lorne was charged in 1600 with 'hering of spreittis and wavering oftentymes fra his wyff, bairnis and familie.' Sometimes he stayed away from home for seven weeks on end, conversing with these bad spirits, who also deceived other families.[58]

[55] cf. J. M. McPherson, op. cit., pp. 129–33.
[56] W. Gregor, op. cit., p. 216.
[57] cf. Cramond, *Records of the Synod of Moray* (Elgin, 1906), p. 94.
[58] cf. *Extracts from the Council Register of the Burgh of Aberdeen*, ed. by John Stuart (Edinburgh, 1871), Vol. II, p. 204. See also J. M. McPherson, op. cit., pp. 129–33.

Fisher folk in Brittany and Normandy loved cemeteries and did not fear them, but they held many superstitions connected with the souls of the departed. For instance there was a fairly common belief in Brittany that the body of a man drowned at sea does not always remain under the water, but comes ashore once a year on All Souls' Day, November 2nd, and takes possession of his empty grave in the churchyard.

Most village cemeteries on the Breton coast contain unoccupied graves, tended carefully in remembrance of men lost at sea. One of the most pathetic of these *cimetières des naufragés* is at Perros-Hamon, near Paimpol, described by Pierre Loti in his novel *Pêcheur d'Islande*. When one stands beside the little grey granite church in the midst of the cemetery, or reads the wording on the mural tablets on either side of the porch, it is easy to believe that the wind soughing in the trees, or the more distant roar of the sea, are the voices of the souls of many a fisherman whose bones lie rotting at the bottom of the ocean within the Arctic Circle or on the Newfoundland Banks, and who seek prayers. Almost all the memorials of the departed at Perros-Hamon refer to '*perdu en Islande*' . . . '*disparu en mer,*' with the prayer '*Qu'ils reposent en paix.*' [59]

Also near Paimpol is the *cimetière des naufragés* at Ploubazlanec, with a long row of graves and the names of countless seafarers who never returned home. Almost every empty grave has a jar of holy water with a sprinkler resting on the turf, also flower vases and wax *immortelles* protected by glass. It needs no great effort of imagination to believe in maritime 'ghosties' in these Breton cemeteries beside the sea, where some of the tombstones are crudely carved with macabre skulls and cross-bones, and other emblems of death. Sometimes the graves are decorated with shells, or with maritime emblems, almost all of them with a cross or crucifix.

West of Morlaix there are many villages with so-called 'parish enclosures,' consisting of the church, an ossuary and a triumphal arch; the latter often highly decorated, symbolising that it is the gateway to heaven. When a churchyard gets too crowded the graves are dug up and the bones put into small niches in the ossuaries, which are sometimes used as funeral chapels. Both the country and the fisher folk like to have cemeteries near at hand, so that they can remember the dead. To the more pious Bretons 'it is not a dismal place of gloomy memories, but a spot where they can sit and smoke

[59] cf. P. F. Anson, *Mariners of Brittany* (1931), p. 126.

and meditate, where one can meet one's friends, where children may play and lovers meet.' [60]

On the Ile-de-Sein—said to have been ruled by Druidesses in pagan times—one is haunted by the presence of death, not only in the old and new cemeteries, but among the rocks on the low shore, and behind the dry-stone walls dividing the tiny fields. The Senans, most of them fishermen, used to believe that once a year the *bag-noz,* or ship of the dead, appeared off the island, blazing with light, and commanded by the sailor who died first within the past twelve months.

When a fisherman died on the Ile-de-Sein, his family invited all the near relatives to a banquet in their small house close-packed in one of the very narrow streets. An oration was pronounced by a guest, after which prayers were recited for the repose of his soul. If a man died away from the island, a cloth was laid on a table in his house, upon which were placed two napkins in the form of a cross. A photograph of the deceased, or if this was lacking, some object belonging to him, was laid in the centre, between two candlesticks and a crucifix All night long a watch was kept up, and prayers recited continuously—a very different sort of 'waukan' to those which took place in many a household on the East Coast of Scotland until well after the middle of the last century.

Prayer for the dead until quite recent times was almost a form of entertainment on this small island out in the Atlantic. Requiem Masses were celebrated frequently. Nearly every morning a priest and an acolyte could be found in the church, hurrying through one or more Offices for the Dead, requested by persons for the repose of the soul of some relative. Another island custom was making a collection on the night of All Saints; the money being used to pay for Masses celebrated for the faithful departed. Four men tolled the church bell, while four others sought alms. One of the latter carried a hand-bell, stopped at each house where a death had occurred recently, and cried out in Breton: *'Christenien difunit, ha lavaromp eun De Profundis evit an annon tremanet!'* ('Christians awake, and pray to God for the souls of the dead, and say for their intentions one *De Profundis!*'). Those inside the house recited the psalm as bidden, the men outside joining in the final *'Requiescat in pace.'*

There were also relics of pagan customs. On some of the older

[60] George Renwick, *Sea-Girt Brittany* (1951), p. 63.

graves one can still see holes carved for libations of milk and wine, though today they are filled with holy water.[61]

In most fishing villages on the coasts of Brittany and Normandy the wives, daughters and mothers of seamen wore, and sometimes still wear, a distinctive head-dress as a sign of mourning. Each district has its own type of *coiffe*. At Tréport, for instance, it was made of black wool without bands. At Berville-sur-Mer, on the estuary of the Seine, fishermen's widows wore a cotton bonnet surrounded by black ribbons. On the Isle of Ushant, the widows and all near female relatives of a seaman put over their coiffes with long floating wings, pleated bonnets. The shawls which covered their shoulders were folded in three. At Saint Cast the fishwives encased their coiffes in a sort of black sheath; but the younger women let the bands of their coiffes fall on the shoulders, the bottoms being decorated with black ribbon.[62]

---

[61] It was not until early in the seventeenth century that a Jesuit priest, Michel le Nobletz, converted the inhabitants of the Ile-de-Sein to the Catholic religion. Until then they had remained half savage pagans, with a sinister reputation as professional wreckers. But for many years after this there was no resident priest on the island, and not until well on in the nineteenth century a regular succession of *curés*.

[62] cf. P. Sébillot, op. cit., pp. 69–70.

ENVOI

ALTHOUGH the fishing industry in all countries is now highly mechanized, concentrated in fewer and fewer ports for economic reasons, it has not lost its romance, and old traditions die hard. In spite of high-speed diesel engines, radar, gyro-compasses, radio-telephones, echo-sounders, nets and ropes made of synthetic fibres, plastic oilskins, and press-button operation of shooting and hauling gear—even what are called 'factory ships'—fishermen are still inclined to be superstitious. I meet young fishermen who surprise me by the way in which they respect the taboos of their grandfathers, even if sometimes they are half ashamed to admit it. In the ever-decreasing number of places where a modified form of old-style working-clothes has survived, also traditional methods of fishing, e.g. the baiting of lines, old customs, taboos and superstitions are not very far buried.

Granted that the average fisherman's home to-day hardly differs from that of the average landsman, and that his shore-going clothes have nothing distinctive about them, nevertheless he remains the same individual below the surface, especially when he practises no religion and is more or less a pagan. This applies equally to the places in France and Scotland mentioned in this book.

It was only three years ago that an octogenarian fisherman on the coast of Banffshire told me that soon after he went to sea as a boy he was quickly cured of a skin disease by one of those magic ointments' which had been prescribed for him by a 'wise woman,' i.e. a reputed witch. Much more recently a twenty year-old fisherman neighbour was obviously scared when he found a priest sitting by the fireside. Later I explained to him that this encounter was unlikely to bring bad luck as he was not going to sea that day. Nothing would induce the skipper of his vessel to start fishing on a Friday, and he can relate stories of all sorts of misfortunes which have befallen men who have done so.

Moreover I incline to think that I have experienced the death omen mentioned on page 151. Eight years ago while the son of a fisherman and myself were both taking an after-dinner nap in adjoining rooms of a house beside the harbour of a Banffshire port, we were awakened by loud and eerie rapping. The noises seemed to be inside the house. I got up, went to the door, but nobody was waiting there. The following day came a letter, telling me that at exactly the same moment as the rapping had been heard, a friend with whom I had been intimate for nearly half a century had died more than five hundred miles away. My companion did not seem surprised, and reminded me that similar death omens had occurred in his family. He did not appear to be the least surprised. These are the facts, believe them or not! [1]

The fisher folk-lore of Northern Europe is still a dormant force to be reckoned with. It is merely adapting itself to changes of environment in this nuclear age.

[1] cf. P. F. Anson, *Abbot Extraordinary* (1958), p. 297.

SELECTED BIBLIOGRAPHY

Alexander, William, *Northern Rural Life* (Edinburgh, 1888).
Anson, P. F., *Fishing Boats and Fisher Folk on the East Coast of Scotland,* (1930).
—— *Fishermen and Fishing Ways* (1931).
—— *Mariners of Brittany* (1931).
—— *The Church and the Sailor* (1949).
—— *Scots Fisher-Folk* (1953).
—— *Christ and the Sailor* (1954).

Baring-Gould, S., *A Book of Folk-Lore* (n.d.).
Bassett, F. S., *Legends of the Sea* (1885).
Benwell, G., and Waugh, A., *Sea Enchantress* (1961).
Bertram, J. G., *The Harvest of the Sea* (1885).
Bosquet, A., *La Normandie romanesque* (Paris, 1845).
Brand, John, *A Brief Description of Orkney, Zetland, etc.* (1701).
Bruce, W., *The Nor'East* (Aberdeen, 1922).
Buchan, Peter, *Annals of Peterhead* (Peterhead, 1819).

Campbell, J. G., *Witchcraft* (Glasgow, 1902).
Caradoc, Th., *Autour les Iles bretonnes* (Paris, n.d.).
Chambers, R., *Domestic Annals of Scotland* (Edinburgh, 1841).
—— *The Book of Days,* Vol. II (1863).
Chevrillon, A., *Derniers reflets à l'Occident* (Paris, 1925).
—— *L'Enchantement breton* (Paris, 1928).
Cramond, William, *The Annals of Banff* (New Spalding Club), 2 vols. (Aberdeen, 1891–3).
—— *The Records of Elgin* (New Spalding Club), 2 vols. (Aberdeen, 1903–7).
—— *The Annals of Cullen* (Banff, 1880).
—— *The Church of Speymouth* (Elgin, 1890).
Cranna, John, *Fisher Life in Buchan* (n.d.).
—— *Fraserburgh, Past and Present* (Aberdeen, 1914).
—— 'Scottish Fisher-Life as it was and is,' in *Chambers' Journal,* July 1899.
Crupples, Mrs., *Newhaven: its Origins and History* (Edinburgh, 1888).

Daleau, F., *Traditions et superstitions de la Gironde* (Bordeaux, 1889).
Dalyell, J. G., *The Darker Superstitions of Scotland* (Edinburgh, 1835).
Deseille, E., *Glossaire du patois des matelots Boulonnais* (Paris, 1884).
Douglas, Andrew, *History of Ferryden* (2nd ed. Montrose, 1857).
Dupuy, A., *Pêcheurs bretons* (Paris, 1920).
Dyer, T. F., Thistleton, *British Popular Customs* (1876).

Edwards, D. H., *Among the Fisher Folks of Usan and Ferryden* (Brechin, 1921).
Elworthy, F. T., *The Evil Eye* (1895).

Folk-Lore Journal, 7 vols. (1883–9).
Folk-Lore Record, 5 vols. (1878–82).

Fraser, Alec, *Northern Folk-Lore on Wells and Water* (Inverness, 1878).
Frazer, J. G., *The Golden Bough*, 3 vols. (1900).

Gourlay, G., *Memories of Cellardyke: or Fisher Life* (Cupar, 1879).
Graham, H. G., *Social Life in Scotland in the Eighteenth Century* (1909).
Gregor, Walter, *Notes on the Folk-Lore of the North-East of Scotland* (1881).
—— *An Echo of the Olden Times from the North-East of Scotland* (Edinburgh, 1874).
—— *Further Report on Folk-Lore in Scotland* (Toronto, 1897).
Guthrie, E. T., *Old Scottish Customs, Local and General* (1885).

Henderson, W., *Notes on the Folk-Lore of Northern Counties* (1879).
Herpin, E., *La Côte d'Emeraude* (Rennes, 1894).
—— *Terreneuvas* (Rennes, 1897).
Holdsworth, E. W. H., *Deep-Sea Fishing and Fishing Boats* (1874).
Hopkins, R. Thurston, *Small Sailing Craft* (1931).
Hutcheson, G., *Days of Yore, or Buckie Past and Present* (Banff, 1887).

Igglesden, C., *Those Superstitions* (1932).

Jeffrey, Alex. (junr.), *Sketches of the traditional history of Burghead* (Aberdeen, 1928).
Jones, W., *Credulities Past and Present* (1880).

La Landelle, G. de, *Moeurs maritimes* (Paris, 1867).
Leatham, James, *Fisher Folk of the North East* (Turriff, 1932).
Le Braz, A., *La Légende de la Mort chez les Bretons* (Paris, 1893).
—— *Pâques d'Islande* (Paris, 1899).
Le Goffic, Ch., *L'Ame bretonne* (Paris, n.d.).
—— *Sur la Côte* (Paris, 1897).
—— *Métiers pittoresques en Bretagne* (Paris, n.d.).
Lentheric, Ch., *Côtes et Ports Français de l'Océan*, 2 vols. (Paris, 1901).

McBain, J. M., *Arbroath: Past and Present* (Arbroath, 1887).
Mackenzie, D. A., *Scottish Folk-Lore* (1935).
Mackinlay, J. M., *Folk-Lore of Scottish Lochs and Springs* (Glasgow, 1893).
Mackintosh, W. R., *Around the Orkney Peat-Fires* (3rd ed. Kirkwall, 1914).
McGibbon, R., *The Fisher Folk of Buchan* (n.d.).
McIver, D., *An Old Fishing Ground: Eyemouth* (Greenock, 1906).
McNeill, F. M., *The Silver Bough*, 4 vols. (Glasgow, 1957).
McPherson, J. M., *Primitive Beliefs in the North-East of Scotland* (1929). (Full list of authorities referred to.)
Mével, Paul, *Les Seigneurs da la Mer* (Paris, 1927).
Miller, Hugh, *Scenes and Legends of the North of Scotland* (Edinburgh, 1855).
Milne, John, *Myths and Superstitions of Buchan District* (Aberdeen, 1881).
Murray, A., *Peterhead a Century Ago* (Peterhead, 1910).
Murray, M. A., *The Witch Cult in Western Europe* (Oxford, 1921).

New Statistical Account of Scotland, 15 vols. (Edinburgh, 1841–5).

Pennant, Thomas, *A Tour of Scotland*, Part I (1769).
Pratt, J. B., *Buchan* (Aberdeen, 1858).

Radford, E. and M., *Encyclopedia of Superstitions* (rev. ed. 1961).
Robertson, Rogers, C., *Social Life in Scotland,* 3 vols. (Edinburgh, 1884–6).

Sawyer, F., *Sussex Natural History, Folk-Lore and Superstitions* (Brighton, 1883).
—— *Supplemental notes on fisheries* (Brighton, 1884).
Sébillot, Paul, *Le Folk-Lore des pêcheurs* (Paris, 1901).
—— *Traditions et superstitions de la Haute-Bretagne* (Paris, 1882).
—— *Légendes, croyances et superstitions de la Mer* (Paris, 1886–7).
—— *Contes populaires de la Haute-Bretagne* (Paris, 1880–2).
—— *Contes des landes et des grèves* (Rennes, 1900).
Sergeant, P. W., *Witches and Warlocks* (1936).
Sharpe, C. Kilpatrick, *Historical Account of Witchcraft in Scotland* (1884).
Shaw, Lachlan, *History of the Province of Moray* (Edinburgh, 1775).
—— Appendix II to *Pennant's Tour in Scotland* (1809).
Simpson, E. B., *Folk-Lore in Scotland* (1908).
Stewart, W. Grant, *The Popular Superstitions and Festive Amusements of the Highlanders of Scotland* (1851).
Summers, Montague, *The History of Witchcraft and Demonology* (1926).
—— *The Geography of Witchcraft* (1927).

Thompson, James, *The Value and Importance of the Scottish Fisheries* (1849).
Tudor, J. R., *The Orkneys and Shetland* (1883).

Vigon, B., 'Folk-Lore de la Mar' in *Archivio,* Vol. VIII.

Witchcraft Detected and Prevented, or the School of Black Art newly opened (Peterhead, 1823).

Young, H. W., *Burghead* (Inverness, 1899).

INDEX

(a) PLACES

(b) SUBJECTS